Attitude-Focused Therapy

In this book, Windy Dryden selects the eight ideas that have had the most influence on him in his career as a psychotherapist, and which form the bedrock of his work.

These ideas reflect both his specific and his general interests in the field. The book offers insight into the author's practice and the theories that have informed his work in a therapeutic setting. It discusses the role that attitudes play in psychologically disturbed and psychologically healthy responses to life's adversities. The book also elaborates the author's views on what promotes psychological change as well as why he considers the concepts of responsibility and choice to be so important in psychotherapy. Finally, the book highlights Windy Dryden's more recent work in the field of single-session therapy.

This accessible and engaging book will be a fascinating read for counsellors and psychotherapists, both in training and in practice.

Windy Dryden, PhD, is Emeritus Professor of Psychotherapeutic Studies at Goldsmiths University of London and is an international authority on Rational Emotive Behaviour Therapy (REBT). He has worked in psychotherapy for over 45 years and is the author and editor of over 250 books.

Attitude-Focused Therapy

8 Influential Ideas in Counselling and Psychotherapy

Windy Dryden

Routledge
Taylor & Francis Group

LONDON AND NEW YORK

First published 2022
by Routledge
2 Park Square, Milton Park, Abingdon, Oxon OX14 4RN

and by Routledge
605 Third Avenue, New York, NY 10158

Routledge is an imprint of the Taylor & Francis Group, an informa business

British Library Cataloguing-in-Publication Data
A catalogue record for this book is available from the British Library

Library of Congress Cataloging-in-Publication Data
A catalog record has been requested for this book

ISBN: 9781032049786 (hbk)
ISBN: 9781032049762 (pbk)
ISBN: 9781003195443 (ebk)

DOI: 10.4324/9781003195443

Typeset in Times New Roman
by Newgen Publishing UK

Contents

Introduction

In this book, I have selected eight ideas that have had the most influence on me in my career as a psychotherapist. These ideas reflect both my specific and my general interests in the field. From a specific perspective, my allegiance has been to the ideas of Albert Ellis since I first encountered them in the mid-1970s. Chapters 2 and 3 are focused on key ideas that stem from Ellis's work.

In Chapter 2, I discuss the role that attitudes play in psychologically disturbed and psychologically healthy responses to life's adversities. Ellis put forward an *ABC* framework where *A* stands for adversity, *B* stands for the beliefs that one holds about the adversity, and *C* stands for the consequences of *A*×*B*. I have never been happy with the term 'belief' as employed by Ellis and had considered for a while that the term 'basic attitude' was more accurate, as I discuss in Chapter 2. So, in 2016, I decided to change it and have used it henceforth (Dryden, 2016). In that publication, I also decided to use the terms 'rigid and extreme' instead of the term 'irrational' and the terms 'flexible and non-extreme' instead of the term 'rational'. So, in Chapter 2, I comprehensively discuss the differences between rigid and extreme basic attitudes and flexible and non-extreme basic attitudes and their impact on responses to adversity.

Having discussed the B in the ABC framework in Chapter 2, in Chapter 3 I discuss the A and C. In particular, I review the concept of 'inference' at A as it relates to the person's personal domain (Beck, 1976) and the consequences of both sets of attitudes at C. Here, I distinguish between a) unhealthy negative emotions vs healthy negative emotions, b) unconstructive vs constructive behaviour and c) highly distorted subsequent thinking that is skewed to the negative and ruminative vs realistic, balanced and non-ruminative thinking.

While Chapters 2 and 3 explain my views on the factors that account for psychological disturbance and health, in Chapters 4 and 5 I discuss ideas that have influenced my views on what promotes psychological change. In Chapter 4, I discuss the concept of responsibility and the importance of people taking responsibility for what they are responsible for and not taking responsibility for what they are not responsible for. The difficulty when discussing this concept with clients is to do so while making it clear that blame is not a part of taking responsibility unless the person chooses to make it so.

In Chapter 5, I focus on the concept of choice and, in particular, what I call the power of the second response. Thus, when a client makes themself anxious, for example in the face of a threat, as therapist I want to help them to respond to that threat with non-anxious concern. However, it should be acknowledged by both of us that the client's first response to the threat is likely to be an anxious one. The idea that the client's power is in their second and subsequent responses shows them that while they may have, at the time, little control over their first response, they can learn to identify and stand back from that first response. This is their second response. They can then access what they learned in therapy about dealing with threat in a concerned but non-anxious way and choose to continue with their first response (which I call 'going with the grain' as it is a natural response for them) or to implement their third and subsequent response, i.e. dealing with the threat with factors that will promote concern rather than anxiety (which I call 'going against the grain' since this is not a natural response for them).

So far, I have discussed influential therapeutic ideas that have a *specific* focus. In Chapter 1, I consider an idea with a more *general* focus. This idea has had an enormous impact on how I think about the practice of therapy and how I practise it in all its forms. This concept is known as the 'working alliance' and in its present form originated in the work of Ed Bordin (1979). In its expanded form (Dryden, 2011), working alliance theory argues that the effectiveness of therapy is dependent in large part on the therapist and client a) having a good therapeutic bond, b) sharing views on salient aspects of therapy, c) agreeing on the objectives of their meeting(s), and d) being able to carry out tasks that jointly facilitate the client achieving their therapeutic goals. If I were to rank the ideas discussed in this book on how influential they have been on my work as therapist, trainer and supervisor, this would occupy joint first place.[1]

I see the working alliance as an umbrella in its overarching effect on the work that I do as a therapist. However, this concept does not have anything to say about the specific ideas that a therapist holds in mind and implements in the course of therapy. Although I have been most closely associated with Rational Emotive Behaviour Therapy (REBT) in my career,[2] I have always held a broad view on matters therapeutic.[3] Thus, I have always been flexible in my REBT practice and influenced by ideas that come from different therapeutic sources. At different times, I have been influenced by eclecticism, integration and recently by work currently being done in therapeutic pluralism (Cooper & McLeod, 2011). However, I have always practised therapy in my own idiosyncratic way. I discuss the concepts of flexibility, pluralism and idiosyncratic practice in Chapter 6.

As I point out in Chapter 7, I have learned most from watching and listening to experienced and skilful therapists practising therapy and from studying transcripts of actual sessions. As such,

I have always resolved to demonstrate therapy when giving a training workshop and, to date, I have done almost 500 demonstration sessions. In doing so, I have learned a lot from the feedback that I have received from members of the workshop audience and from studying transcripts of my own of these sessions.

Finally, in Chapter 8 I discuss ideas from the field of single-session therapy (SST) which latterly have had a profound influence on my thinking about how to respond to requests for therapeutic help at the point of need and how to distribute fairly therapeutic resources to those who request them in a community. In furthering the single-session mindset and mode of service delivery, I have recently run many workshops and training sessions in single-session therapy, given that SST does not regularly feature on the curriculum of university training courses in counselling and psychotherapy. In my view, all therapists need to be equipped to deal with therapeutic situations where clients want to be helped quickly and do not want to enter into an ongoing therapeutic relationship, and I want to play a part in helping them to be thus equipped.

Windy Dryden
London and Eastbourne
June 2021

Notes

1   The other idea in joint first place would be the role of attitudes in psychological disturbance and health.
2   Ideas related to REBT can be found in Chapters 2–5 of this book.
3   I am fortunate to have had a broad therapeutic education at a formative part of my career on the MSc Psychotherapy course at the University of Warwick (1978–1980) directed by Drs John and Marcia Davis.

Chapter 1

The working alliance

Overview

The working alliance between the therapist and client is a pantheoretical idea that has had a very significant impact on my professional career. In this opening chapter, I will describe its four main components and discuss elements of each component that I have found particularly helpful. I show how these four components are interdependent and discuss ruptures to the alliance and how I tend to address them. I end the chapter with a discussion of 'feedback-informed therapy', a recent approach designed to help the therapist better tailor therapy to the client.

Introduction

In 1978, I enrolled in a two-year part-time MSc in Psychotherapy course at the University of Warwick run by John and Marcia Davis. By this time, I had already trained as an REB therapist, but I thought that I needed more rounded training in psychotherapy, which is what I got at Warwick. I was introduced to several important therapeutic ideas during those two years, but none more important than the 'working alliance'. The person behind the concept was a man named Ed Bordin, whose interests were

DOI: 10.4324/9781003195443-1

in vocational decision-making and what came to be known as working alliance theory (Constantino, Ladany & Borkovec, 2010). In the late 1970s, Bordin published a paper that influenced me profoundly (Bordin, 1979). Bordin (1983: 35) later defined the working alliance as 'a collaboration for change for which I have identified three aspects: (1) mutual agreements and understandings regarding the *goals* sought in the change process; (2) the *tasks* of each of the partners; and (3) the bonds between the partners necessary to sustain the enterprise'.

Goals, tasks, bonds

In looking back at these two papers, I am struck by the order in which Bordin described these three components. In both publications, it is: goals, tasks, and bonds, whereas in my early work I represent them in the order: bonds, goals, and tasks (Dryden, 1982, 1986).

Bordin seems to be saying that what brings the therapist and client together is their respective goals. Put broadly, the client seeks relief of their suffering, and the therapist seeks to relieve that suffering. Assuming that both parties agree on their respective goals in ways that are personal to the client, then the tasks that both undertake are important in determining whether or not the client will achieve their goals. For Bordin, the quality of the bond between therapist and client influences the sustainability of the work both have come together to do.

In reflecting on Bordin's (1983) definition, I think that this underestimates Bordin's opinion of the importance of the bonds component of the alliance. Indeed, in their appreciation piece on Bordin, Constantino et al. (2010) note that Bordin distinguished between bonds that result from collaboration and bonds that contribute to collaboration. For Bordin, they say, it was the latter type of bonds that was so central to therapeutic change. My view is that this distinction reflects Bordin's psychoanalytic interests. For therapists of this persuasion, it is the resolution of transferential conflict that gets played out in the therapy room that is so healing. This resolution allows the client to collaborate with the therapist in the pursuit of their goals, which presumably they could not do before such resolution. This latter situation pre-dated the subsequent work that has been done on the importance of the therapist identifying and healing ruptures to the alliance when they occur. Again, it is the healing of such breaches that is regarded as a significant therapeutic change factor.

I will discuss the healing of ruptures in greater depth later in the chapter.

Views

From the outset, I sensed that something was missing from Bordin's tripartite model of the working alliance. After much thought, I realised that the missing component was what I call 'views' (see Dryden, 2006, 2011). These are the understandings that the therapist and client have about salient aspects of therapy. These aspects range from the practical (e.g. confidentiality, cancellation policy, fees, etc.) to the psychological (e.g. what determines and maintains the client's problem(s) and what will resolve the client's issue(s)). When I discuss my own four-component version of the working alliance, I do so in the order: bonds, views, goals, and tasks. In doing so, I am saying that, after the early development of a bond, if the therapist and client share common views on salient practical and psychological aspects of therapy, then they will proceed, and if they lack such agreed understandings, then they probably won't. In which case, the therapist's job is to refer the client to a practitioner whose views better match the client's views.

Having introduced Bordin's working alliance model with my later addition, I will now consider each of the four components of the alliance separately. Please bear in mind, however, that, in reality, these components are interdependent, an important point that I will address later.

Bonds

Therapeutic bonds refer to the interpersonal interconnectedness between therapist and client. In my work, I have found several elements of the bond important to take into consideration. I will now discuss these elements.

The importance of the client feeling safe in the therapeutic relationship

In workshops when I describe the importance of the client feeling safe in the therapeutic relationship, I invite an audience to imagine what it would be like for them not to feel safe with their therapist. What impact would feeling unsafe have on that relationship? Most people in the audience say that they would not return to therapy.[1] I then ask them to imagine staying in therapy while feeling unsafe. What would they do to try to feel safe under such conditions? Responses range from 'not disclosing relevant material to the therapist' to 'pretending to be better than one feels' and 'trying to make the therapist feel good to ward off threats to their safety'. As can be imagined, none of these activities is likely to promote a positive outcome from therapy. Indeed, they are more likely to be markers of a poor therapeutic outcome.

So what can the therapist do to help the client feel safe in the relationship? The primary way in which the therapist can do this is by showing the client that they are trustworthy.

Being trustworthy

Being trustworthy involves the therapist:

- being congruent with the client so that the client knows that the therapist is not hiding behind a façade (see later)
- being reliable in the sense that they will do what they say they will do (e.g. they abide by their confidentiality policy)

- showing that they accept the client as the client is (see later)
- holding professional boundaries (Sometimes a client will test trust by inviting the therapist to break a professional boundary. Showing the client that they will not do this and tactfully explaining why helps to build trust.)
- focusing on what the client's goals are (see later)
- striving to demonstrate that they understand the client from the client's frame of reference (see later)
- demonstrating professional expertise (Here the therapist will communicate that they know what they are talking about, but will also say, 'I don't know,' if this is the case.)
- encouraging the client to work with the therapist as an equal partner in a team (see below).

Teamwork

I mentioned that encouraging the client to work with the therapist as an equal partner in a team is an important way in which a therapist can demonstrate that they are trustworthy.

I think that it is important to be honest about what the therapist and client bring to the team. The therapist brings expertise in a particular perspective on psychological problems and their remediation and how best to engage the client and maintain this engagement throughout the therapeutic process. The client brings their expertise on their own experience and a host of inner resources which it is vital that the therapist identifies and works with in therapy.

Therapists from different orientations will have different perspectives on therapeutic teamwork and how to promote it. My six months of training at the Center for Cognitive Therapy in Philadelphia in 1981 shaped my views on this issue in two main ways:

- establishing a problem list with the client
- developing with the client an agenda for each therapy session.

Establishing a problem list

A problem list is a list of the client's problems that they would like to deal with in therapy. It is developed at the beginning of the therapeutic process and helps both therapist and client keep up to date with what the client is struggling with and ensures that an item does not get neglected. Thus, the list includes all the problems that the client wants to address in therapy. It is important to recognise that once developed this list is not fixed and the client will want to add to and subtract from the list items as therapy proceeds.

If a therapist is to help the client to develop a problem list, I think that it is important to deter the client from 'problem hopping'. When this happens, the client brings up a different problem each week so that there is little continuity between therapy sessions. The role of the therapist here is to ensure that the client works on a problem with which they are currently preoccupied and to encourage the client to deal with that issue until it is no longer a problem, unless there is a valid reason to do otherwise.

Developing a session agenda

Establishing a session agenda is a useful way of fostering teamwork and helps both therapist and client to utilise session time efficiently. Using session agendas originated in the pioneering work of Beck, Rush, Shaw & Emery (1979) on the cognitive therapy of depression. It involves the therapist doing the following:

Providing a rationale for the use of session agendas. Here, the therapist explains that setting a session agenda at the beginning of the session:

- helps the client choose how to spend time in the session and ensures that they are devoting the most time to their most pressing issue
- ensures that the therapist and client are 'on the same page' during the session

- provides the therapist with an opportunity to cover important issues such as reviewing past homework tasks and negotiating new tasks to enable the client to get the most from therapy between sessions
- after covering these points, the therapist encourages the client to raise any reservations they may have concerning the use of an agenda-based approach to sessions. To encourage teamwork, the therapist takes seriously any concerns expressed by the client and responds with tact and respect. If the client is still doubtful, the therapist will suggest that they try setting a session agenda and using it so that the client experiences it in action. If the client finds it unhelpful, then the therapist will dispense with it going forward.

Explaining what a session agenda covers. A session agenda usually includes the following:

- the client's report on any assignment that the client has agreed to do in the preceding week
- the problem the client wants to focus on most during the session
- any additional issues the client wants to discuss
- an assignment based on what was covered in the session that the client agrees to do before the next session
- the client's feedback on the session that they have just had.

Creating and maintaining the reflection process

A third way of encouraging teamwork in therapy is for the therapist to initiate and maintain a channel of communication which I have referred to as the 'reflection process' in my writings (e.g. Dryden, 1989). As the name suggests, the reflection process is a process where the therapist and client stand back from the main action, as it were, and reflect on what has been happening in as objective a manner as they can. Some therapeutic approaches distinguish between the 'experiencing ego' and the 'observer ego' where the observer part of a client can gain some distance from the experiences of the experiencing part of themself to understand these experiences better (Sterba, 1934). I find this distinction useful when providing a rationale to clients for the use of the reflection process.

Once the therapist has provided a rationale for the use of the reflection process, as before they encourage the client to voice any reservations they may have about using such a method and respond to any concerns expressed. If the client does not find this way of working helpful, then the therapist will refrain from its use.

Typically, items referred to in the reflection process are issues experienced by either party as problematic that warrant more objective discussion. As with agenda-setting, the therapist provides a rationale for the creation of this mode of communication.

The 'core conditions'

Perhaps the most influential idea in the entire field of psychotherapy is one that is generally known as the 'core conditions' (Rogers, 1957). Rogers argued that when the client experienced the therapist as empathic, congruent and demonstrating an attitude of unconditional positive regard, then constructive therapeutic change would inevitably happen. Furthermore, Rogers argued that these conditions were necessary and sufficient for such change to occur. Ellis (1959) disagreed with Rogers and argued that while such conditions might be desirable, they were neither necessary nor sufficient to promote change.

My view is that it is important for the client to feel understood by their therapist and accepted by them and that they would prefer the therapist to be transparent rather than hiding behind a façade. For some clients, these conditions are all they require, while for others additional therapeutic ingredients need to be present. For example, if a person seeks therapy for a specific phobia or OCD, then the experience of the core conditions may help them to engage in more focused therapy tasks (e.g. exposure and response prevention). However, without such task engagement, the impact of the core conditions will be minimal.

Interactive stances

A key aspect of the therapeutic bond is, in my opinion, the interactive stance that the therapist adopts with the client. In my view, whichever stance the therapist adopts, it is important that they preserve the engagement and activity of the client. In my view, this is best done when therapy takes the form of a conversation between the therapist and the client (Hobson, 1985). I adopt three major interactive stances in my work with clients which I will discuss below.

Active listening

When I adopt an active listening stance, I aim to encourage the client to talk and explore their concerns and to communicate my understanding of what the client is saying as they relate their narrative. This is, of course, empathic understanding, one of Rogers' (1957) core conditions. I have never understood why person-centred therapy developed by Rogers (1942) 80 years ago was ever referred to as non-directive, as in his demonstration sessions he is actively focused on striving to understand the moment-by-moment experiences (feelings and meanings) of the client.

Active intervening

When I adopt an active intervening stance, I aim to help the client to focus on their most pressing concern. Having understood this problem from their frame of reference, I offer my frame of reference which is usually informed by the *ABC* framework of Rational

Emotive Behaviour Therapy (Dryden, 2016). If this makes sense to them, I use the framework as a way of helping them deal with their problem and achieve their goal (see Chapter 2).

Prompting

When I adopt a prompting interactive stance, it is usually once the client has learned the skills of helping themself and I want to encourage them to take the lead in applying these skills to whatever issue they wish to discuss. This helps them to become their own therapist and is usually a precursor to the winding down of sessions or the end of therapy.

Therapeutic style

I see therapeutic style as different from therapeutic stance in that the same stance can be taken using different styles. Thus, when a therapist adopts an active intervening style, they can do so using a formal or an informal style. My late friend and colleague Arnold Lazarus (1989) argued that, ideally, the therapist should be prepared to vary their therapeutic style to meet the preferences and expectations of the client. However, they should only do this genuinely. Lazarus (1993) referred to this as the therapist becoming an 'authentic chameleon'. My therapeutic style preferences are 'informal', 'humorous' and self-disclosing, although I am prepared to adopt formal, serious and non-self-disclosing styles when appropriate.

The therapist's influence base

A different way of looking at the therapist–client bond stems from the application of social psychological concepts to psychotherapy, which was particularly in vogue in the 1980s (e.g. Dorn, 1984). Here the focus is on therapy as a process of social influence. Therapists, in general, would prefer to see themselves as facilitators rather than influencers. Having said that, if one takes the view that the therapist is trying to influence the client to live a psychologically healthier and more resourceful life, then influence may be more acceptable. When one takes this view, the issue then becomes whether the client is most likely to listen to and be influenced by the therapist if they like the therapist or if they are impressed by the therapist's level of expertise, or a combination of these two factors. My view is that the therapist should undertake to identify the client's influence preferences and make use of these if possible.

Transference and counter-transference

In therapy, the term 'transference' refers to a situation where the client redirects their feelings for a significant person in their life, usually a parent, to the therapist. The goal of the therapist is to use the client's emotions to help them learn more about their conflicts.

The term 'counter-transference' refers to a situation where the therapist experiences feelings towards the client. These feelings may reflect a position where the therapist redirects their feelings for a significant person in their own life to the client or a situation where the therapist can learn something valuable about what the client is attempting to elicit in them.

When these phenomena occur in therapy, my practice is to refer them to the reflection process (see above) and encourage the client to stand back and join me in exploring the issues that emerge.

Views

The 'views' component of the working alliance is one that I introduced because I considered that the tri-partite model of the alliance put forward by Bordin (1979) omitted a vital part of the partnership between therapist and client. By 'views' I mean the collection of perspectives and understandings that both parties have about salient aspects of psychotherapy. These range from the practical to the psychological.

One of my clients was concurrently seeing a marital therapist with her husband. She had to be hospitalised, and during her hospital stay she requested a marital therapy session with her husband and their therapist, which they had. When she received the therapist's bill for the session, she was outraged. He had charged her three times his usual rate. When she challenged him on it, he replied that as it took him an hour to get to the hospital and an hour to get back, those two journeys plus the hour-long counselling session amounted to the equivalent of three hours of his professional time – hence his invoice. Now, one might argue with this therapist concerning his billing practice, but my point is that this man's error was that he did not inform my client in advance what it would cost the couple to have a therapy session with him in hospital. If he had, then she would have had the choice of having the session or not. If she had chosen to have the session, it would have been with the full knowledge of how much the therapist was to bill the couple. However, this did not happen. What did happen was that the client refused to pay two-thirds of the bill, and the counsellor refused to reduce the bill. This impasse led the client and her husband to stop her couples counselling sessions.

This situation came to pass, in my opinion, for two reasons. First, it was because my client and the therapist had different views concerning what constituted his professional billable time. He counted travel time to and from the hospital as part of his time, while she only counted the session in this way. Second, they felt that they could not compromise on their positions.

I believe this story teaches us several points concerning the importance of views:

- The therapist and client are likely to hold views about a variety of issues that concern psychotherapy.
- If these views are different, this difference will serve as a potential alliance rupture.

- However, it is not the difference of views that is problematic. Instead, it is the therapist and the client's collective failure to resolve this difference that ruptures the alliance.

With these points in mind, let me discuss the practical and psychological views that I mentioned earlier.

Practical views

Here is a list of practical views relevant to psychotherapy on which it is important that the therapist and client agree:

- the therapist's confidentiality policy
- the therapist's fees and how they should be paid
- the therapist's cancellation policy
- the length of counselling sessions.

Psychological views

Perhaps the most important role that the 'views' component plays in the working alliance concerns the therapist's and client's views concerning:

- making sense of the client's problems and
- what constitutes effective therapy for these problems.

Making sense of the client's problems

An old colleague of mine at the University of Aston in Birmingham, Chris Barker, did some important work in the early 1990s concerning lay people's views of psychological problems and the implications for treatment. Barker and his co-researchers argued that when a person's views about psychological problems were consistent with those of a therapy approach, if the person had that therapy, then the resultant working alliance would be stronger than if they had therapy which did not match these views (Barker, Pistrang, Shapiro & Shaw, 1990; Pistrang & Barker, 1992). A certain amount of difference in these respective views is certainly not a problem and may be anticipated. However, if a person seeking help holds a radically different view about the reason why they have psychological problems from those embedded in a therapeutic approach, then in all probability the person would not be helped by such an approach.

Imagine, for example, a person who holds a psychodynamic view of their psychological problems being referred for CBT, which has a different view of such problems. There will be tension in the alliance and unless the therapist and client can come to a shared understanding on this issue, then the client would be better served by an approach to therapy with a closer match to their views on this point.

What constitutes effective therapy for the client's problems

Many years ago when I worked in Birmingham, a man rang me and asked me if I practised an approach to therapy known as RT. I practise Rational Emotive Behaviour Therapy (REBT), which was originally known as rational therapy (RT), and I thought that the man was referring to REBT but in its earliest form. On the basis of that misunderstanding, I agreed to see him. However, it soon transpired that he was seeking Reichian Therapy (RT), a body-work oriented therapy that is very different from REBT! What did I do? I referred him to a person I know who practised Reichian Therapy. I did not try to persuade him to change his help-seeking preferences since he was quite definite about what he was looking for.

A client and therapist may have a shared view of the client's problems, but a different view on how they can be changed. Thus, a client's views of their problems may match CBT's views on this issue, but they may think that understanding the origin of their dysfunctional attitudes will lead to therapeutic change, whereas the CBT view of effective therapy is very different. Again, unless the client and therapist can negotiate a shared view here, effective therapy will be compromised.

Informed consent

A client can be said to have given informed consent when they have understood salient aspects of therapy and have agreed to proceed on the basis of that understanding. While different clients will require different amounts of information before giving their informed consent, what they need to know will be drawn from the topics I have discussed in the two sections above.

Goals

Goals are the raison d'être of psychotherapy. Clients generally seek therapy because they are in some kind of emotional pain and are looking for relief from that pain. That is why, when asked what they want to achieve from therapy, many clients give 'relief from pain' answers. Thus, they say things like 'I don't want to feel anxious' or 'I want to feel happy'. Such answers, while understandable from the client's perspective, are too vague to be helpful and the therapist needs to help them to set goals that are clear enough for them to aim for.

From an alliance perspective, it is crucial for the therapist and client to agree on goals. Otherwise, the client may want to achieve one set of goals and the therapist may want them to achieve another, and this will lead to problems in the alliance.

There are several reasons why a client and their therapist may have different ideas about the client's goals. First, clients are often more conservative about their goals than the goals their therapists have for them. Clients are often content to leave therapy earlier than their therapists think they should (Maluccio, 1979).

Second, clients may be guided by 'relief of pain' goals, while therapists are more likely to be guided by goals that involve clients resolving issues which are often more ambitious than 'relief from pain' goals. In fact, I think that it is important to distinguish between 'relief from pain' goals and what Mahrer (1967) calls 'overcoming disturbance' goals. Clients who want to be free from emotional pain tend to leave therapy having achieved these 'relief from pain' goals. However, they may still be vulnerable to such pain because they have not resolved the issues underlying their pain. They have not overcome their disturbance and do not have overcoming disturbance goals. When therapists are successful at encouraging clients to work towards overcoming disturbance, they are helping these clients to 'get better' rather than 'feel better', a distinction made by Albert Ellis (1972) about half a century ago.

I mentioned Mahrer (1967) earlier. Based on a survey of contributors to his classic edited book entitled *The Goals of Psychotherapy*, Mahrer distinguished between overcoming disturbance goals and promoting growth goals. Thus, the third reason why the client and therapist may have differences about the client's goals is that the therapist wants to promote the client's development and the client wants to overcome their disturbance.

Addressing obstacles to effective goal negotiation

When negotiating goals with a client, I have found that it is worth taking time to help the client set a realistic goal. However, there are a number of obstacles to surmount while effectively negotiating such a goal.

When a client sets a vague goal

If a client sets a vague goal, it is important to help them to make this goal as specific as possible. Examples of vague goals are: 'I want to be happy', 'I want to get over my anxiety' and 'I want to get on with my life'. I find it useful in this respect to implement a commonly used acronym which is an antidote to vague goals. It is SMART. Smart goals are those that are: specific, measurable, attainable, realistic and timely.

When the client wants to change an adversity

A client may wish to change the adversity that features in their problem rather than changing their unconstructive responses to the adversity to those that are constructive. If this is the case and the adversity can be changed, I help them to understand that the best chance they have to change the adversity is when they are in a healthy frame of mind to do so, and this is achieved when their responses to this adversity are constructive. So, before they can change the adversity, the client needs to change their disturbed responses to the adversity.

When the client wants to change another person

When the client wants to change another person, I help them to understand that this goal is inappropriate as the behaviour of others is not under their direct control. However, attempts to influence others are under the client's direct control and *may* lead to such behavioural change. As such, these influence attempts are appropriate goals, but again they need to be pursued once they are in a healthy state of mind.

It is also important to help the client consider their responses when their influence attempts do not work. Helping clients to deal constructively with such failed attempts is often important in such cases.

When the client sets a goal based on experiencing less of the problematic response

Often, when asked about their goals in relation to the adversity, a client may say that they want to feel less of the disturbed emotion (called an unhealthy negative emotion) that is featured in their problem (e.g. less anxious). If this happens, I invite them to consider striving to experience instead a healthy negative emotion of relative intensity to the unhealthy negative emotion, rather than striving to experience an unhealthy negative emotion of decreased intensity. Since the adversity is negative, their choice is to feel healthily bad or unhealthily bad.

When the client sets a goal based on experiencing the absence of the problematic response

A client may nominate the absence of the problem as their goal (e.g. 'I don't want to feel anxious when giving a talk'). My response is that it is not possible to live in a response vacuum and from there I discuss the presence of a set of healthy responses to their adversity as their goal.

When your client sets as a goal a positive response to the actual situation and bypasses the adversity

Another situation that may well occur when the therapist asks the client for their goal is that the client may nominate a positive response to the actual situation while bypassing the adversity within that situation. For example, if a client says, 'I want to become confident at giving public presentations', when he is anxious about saying something foolish when he talks, then he bypasses dealing with the adversity. My response to this client would be to ask the person how he could become confident at giving public presentations when he was anxious about saying something foolish. By helping this client to deal with the adversity first and to set an appropriate goal with respect to that adversity, I would be helping him to take an important first step in his path towards increasing his confidence about his performance. If he does not take this step, then he is unlikely to achieve his nominated goal of becoming confident at giving public presentations.

When a client wants to feel indifferent in the face of an adversity

Sometimes a client says that their goal is not to care about a particular adversity when, in reality, they do care about it. Indeed, their disturbed feelings indicate that they do care. My practice is to help my client understand what not caring or indifference means and then help them to see that the only way they can achieve this is to adopt an attitude of indifference which involves lying to themselves. When the client understands this, they tend to drop this as a goal.

When a client nominates a goal that is dangerous or unrealistic

Sometimes a client nominates a goal that is, in Law and Jacob's (2015) terms, 'unacceptable'. What they mean is that the goal is either 'dangerous (e.g. a person with anorexia wanting to set a goal to lose weight, or someone with depression wanting to be helped to end their life), or...unrealistic (e.g. someone with a physical disability wanting to be a professional footballer)' (Law & Jacob, 2015: 16). As Law and Jacob (2015) go on to say, these goals should not be dismissed, but they should be a prelude for discussion and careful re-negotiation. Helping the client to imagine responding to a friend who nominates such goals can be particularly helpful here in providing the client with sufficient distance to enable them to participate in their own goal re-negotiation with the therapist.

Tasks

The fourth component of the working alliance model is tasks – activities carried out by the therapist and the client which are goal-directed in nature. Such tasks may be broad in nature (e.g. to engage in the task of self-exploration in person-centred therapy) or more specific (e.g. to engage in Socratic dialogue in cognitive-behaviour therapy).

From a working alliance perspective, the emphasis is not on the content of such tasks, but on a number of issues related to their implementation. In my view with respect to tasks, the working alliance between the therapist and client is enhanced under the following conditions:

- when the client understands that they have therapeutic tasks to perform and they know the nature of these tasks
- when the client understands that performing these tasks will help them to achieve their goals
- when the client recognises that they have to work to change. If the client thinks that they all they need to do to change is to attend therapy sessions, then they will not, in all probability, achieve their goals
- when the client has the capability to carry out the therapeutic tasks required of them
- when the client has the necessary skills to carry out the therapeutic tasks required of them.

A client can generally learn the skills to carry out certain therapeutic tasks if they have the time to do so, but if they do not have the capability to carry them out, then it is the job of the therapist to find and suggest tasks that they can carry out:

- when the client has a certain level of confidence to execute relevant tasks
- when the tasks that the client is called upon to carry out have sufficient therapeutic potency to help the client to achieve their goals. The research literature will guide the therapist in their choice of tasks that the client needs to carry out here
- when the client is prepared to carry out these tasks. Just because a task is therapeutically potent, it does not follow that the client will be prepared to implement it. It is the therapist's job here to help the client to voice their doubts, reservations

and objections (DROs) to carrying out the task and to address these DROs. If the client will still not implement the task, the therapist should help the client to find a different task that they are prepared to implement even though it may be less therapeutically potent than the original task
- when the client understands the nature of the therapist's tasks and how these relate to their tasks and goals
- when the client is in a sufficiently good frame of mind to execute their tasks.

Tasks and the therapist's expertise

How much of the effectiveness of therapy is dependent on the therapist's expertise? This factor accounts for a small, but reliable, amount of the outcome variance (Baldwin & Imel, 2013; Beutler, Malik, Alimohammed, Harwood, Talebi, Noble, & Wong, 2004). Here is a sample of the issues that pertain to the therapist's expertise in implementing tasks.

Therapist skill

When the therapist is skilful in implementing tasks, they are able to do so with clarity and with due regard for the client in front of them. It is the difference between offering the client bespoke therapy versus expecting the client to fit into a predetermined way of working. There are many tasks where the therapist needs to demonstrate skill. Here is a small sample.

Explaining one's approach to therapy and gaining informed consent. Before the client can be expected to give their consent to become a client and proceed, they need to know something of the approach to therapy adopted by the therapist. Knowing how much description to give a client and at what level is a skill the therapist needs to demonstrate if they are going to give the client sufficient information to enable them to give their informed consent and if they are going to engage the client productively at the beginning of therapy.

Making judicious referrals. My late friend and colleague Arnold Lazarus (1989) argued that one of the most underrated of therapist skills is that of making judicious referrals. In order to make such a referral, the therapist first needs to conclude that they are not the best person to help the client. This, in itself, requires the therapist to have a degree of humility to know that they can't help everyone and that other therapists are more skilled than they are in helping certain types of clients. Having made this decision, the therapist needs to put this to the client so that the client does not 'feel' rejected, but instead hopeful that the practitioner to whom the therapist has referred the client will be able to help them.

Varying the use of tasks. A skilful therapist needs to be able to vary their tasks according to the client. I find Lazarus's (1989) modality framework of BASIC ID helpful here (see Table 1.1)

Table 1.1   The BASIC ID framework (Lazarus, 1989)

B = Behaviour
A = Affect
S = Sensation
I = Imagery
C = Cognition
I = Interpersonal
D = Drugs/Biology

Clients differ concerning which modalities they favour and which they struggle with. Skilful therapists use tasks that are selected to 'play' to a client's strengths and avoid their weaknesses. Thus, a client who favours 'imagery' and 'behaviour' would do better using tasks that call upon these modalities than tasks that do not. Therapists who have a broad perspective on therapeutic tasks and the flexibility to draw upon this range will strengthen the working alliance more successfully than therapists who do not demonstrate these qualities in their therapy practice.

Helping clients to get the most out of their tasks

For the working alliance to be strong in the task domain of the alliance, the client needs to implement their tasks as well as possible. To this end, the therapist may need to help the client to get the most from these tasks. The therapist can do so by doing the following:

- explaining clearly to the client what their tasks are and answering any questions they have about these tasks
- helping the client to see clearly the relationship between their tasks and their goals. Once the therapist has done this, they need to encourage the client to keep this connection clearly in mind during therapy
- modifying the tasks after taking into account the client's strengths and weaknesses. The therapist can do this before the client carries out their tasks and also after they have done so. In the latter case, the therapist can suggest modifications to the tasks based on the client's feedback on their attempts to perform the tasks
- training the client in these tasks if relevant
- identifying and problem-solving any obstacles to client task execution
- having alternative client tasks in mind if the client refuses to or cannot carry out their original tasks
- when negotiating any homework assignments with the client, making sure that the client specifies what they are going to do, when they are going to do it and how often, and then problem-solving possible obstacles to homework completion.

The interdependent nature of the four components of the working alliance

So far in this chapter I have discussed the four components of the working alliance as if they were separate. However, in reality, they are interdependent and in this section of the chapter I will briefly discuss how the components of the alliance affect one another.

- When the therapist and client have a good relationship in the *bond* domain, it can have a positive effect on the commitment a client may have to engaging with their therapeutic *tasks*.
- If the client and therapist share common *views* on salient aspects of therapy, this can strengthen their *bond*.
- When the client and therapist agree on the *goals* of therapy, this may also strengthen their *bond*.
- When the therapist helps the client to keep their therapeutic *goals* at the forefront of their mind, this encourages the client to implement their *tasks* both within and between sessions when these tasks are goal-directed.
- When the therapist and client agree on the factors that account for the existence of the client's problem (agreement on *views*), they will tend to agree on what constitutes a healthy alternative to these problems (agreement on *goals*).
- When the client and therapist have a shared understanding of their respective *tasks* (agreement on *views*), they will both tend to carry out these *tasks* more effectively then if they did not have such agreement.

The importance of healing alliance ruptures

Therapy, like the course of true love, does not always run smoothly and ruptures sometimes appear in the working alliance. The important point is not that ruptures occur in the alliance, but how they are dealt with. In my view, such ruptures are dealt with in therapy as they are dealt with in any other meaningful relationship, with the exception being that in therapy, in my view, it is the therapist's responsibility to initiate the healing.

Ruptures can occur in any domain of the alliance

Problems can occur in any domain of the working alliance and as the four components of the alliance are interdependent, as discussed above, what may appear to be a rupture in one domain may actually be a rupture in another. I will discuss ruptures whose source lies in the client 'feeling' that they are not getting what they want from therapy or are getting what they don't want.

Bond-related ruptures

Perhaps the most common domain in which a rupture in the alliance occurs is the bond domain. Here are some examples:

- The client does not trust the therapist.
- The client does not 'feel' understood by the therapist.
- The client 'feels' that the therapist does not accept them.
- The client 'feels' that the therapist is putting on an act and is not genuine.
- The client has a negative reaction to the therapist's interpersonal style, for example when a client values autonomy and 'feels' constrained by the interpersonal style of the therapist.
- The client likes the therapist but is sceptical of the therapist's expertise.
- The client values the therapist's expertise but is turned off by the therapist's interpersonal manner.
- The client prefers a more formal (or informal) style of interaction than the therapist provides.
- The client experiences the therapist's humour as inappropriate or disrespectful.
- The client develops a negative (or an overly positive) transference reaction to the therapist.

View-related ruptures

While the therapist and client may disagree on one or more practical issues, I will focus here on examples of ruptures stemming
from lack of agreement in the views domain of the alliance.

- The client disagrees with the therapist's views on their problems
  and what factors maintain these problems.
- The client disagrees with the therapist's views on how best to
  tackle the client's problems.

The main issue here is that not that such disagreements exist, but
that the therapist fails to address them.

Goal-related ruptures

Psychotherapy is a purposive activity and works best when the
client and therapist agree on the client's goals. Ruptures, therefore,
can centre on goal disagreements. Here are some examples.

- The client and therapist disagree on the client's outcome goals.
- The client 'feels' that the therapist wants them to pursue goals
  that they do not have.
- The client has more conservative goals than the therapist has
  for them.
- The therapist asks the client to specify goals before the client
  is ready to do so.

Task-related ruptures

As I have already mentioned, tasks are what the therapist and client
do in order to address the client's problems. Task-related ruptures
can be due to the following:

- The client does not know what they are supposed to do in
  therapy and the therapist does not help them in this respect.

- The client disagrees with their therapy tasks, but the therapist proceeds as if they agree with them.
- The client does not have the ability to implement their therapy tasks, but the therapist proceeds as if they do have this ability.
- The client does not have the skills to implement their therapy tasks, but the therapist proceeds as if they do have these skills.
- The therapist pushes the client to do things in therapy that they are not ready to do or that they find overwhelming to do.
- The client does not understand what the therapist's tasks are in therapy and the therapist does not help them in this respect.

How clients express ruptures

Safran and Muran (2000) distinguished between two types of alliance ruptures: alliance ruptures based on client withdrawal and alliance ruptures based on client confrontation.

In withdrawal ruptures, the client demonstrates withdrawal in one or more of several ways. They may disengage from the therapist and/or the therapeutic process. In addition, the client may disengage from their own emotions. When a rupture is based on withdrawal, the client will probably have difficulty expressing why therapy is not working for them. If they do express it, they will probably blame themself rather than point to anything that the therapist is doing or failing to do. Otherwise, they may appear cooperative and say that they are benefiting from therapy when they are clearly not.

With confrontation ruptures, by their very nature, the rupture is more obvious than with a withdrawal rupture. Here the client is more direct in expressing their negative feelings towards the therapist and/or about salient aspects of the therapy or therapeutic process. The client directly expresses anger or resentment, as well as dissatisfaction with regard to the therapist or certain aspects of the therapy.

When a confrontation rupture occurs, the client attacks the therapist and it is perhaps understandable if the therapist reacts in a defensive way to the client. It is important for the therapist to learn to stand back from such attacks and engage the client in the reflection process concerning their dissatisfactions with the therapist and/or the therapy process.

Dealing with alliance ruptures in therapy

While the therapist needs to respond to confrontation ruptures in a different way from withdrawal ruptures, in this section I will discuss strategies that the therapist can use that are common to both.

- The therapist notices behaviour on the part of the client which they interpret to be a sign of a rupture to the alliance.
- The therapist invites the client to stand back and access the reflection process with them.
- The therapist describes this behaviour to the client, avoiding making any inferences about the client's behaviour.
- The therapist invites the client to comment on the therapist's observations. In doing so, the therapist encourages the client to express their negative feelings about the therapeutic relationship and/or the therapeutic process.
- If the client finds it difficult to express such negative feelings, the therapist should explore the client's fears about doing so and work with them to address their fears and then express their true feelings that underpin the rupture.
- It is important for the therapist to accept responsibility for their part in the alliance rupture and to admit any mistakes that they have made. In this sense, it is important for the therapist to apologise to the client for the mistake.
- If the client's feelings towards the therapist are transferential in nature, the therapist should first accept such feelings but then find a way to help the client understand the connection between the therapist and the person or persons that the client has conflictual feelings towards. This should be done in such a way that the client can explore this connection rather than feeling ashamed for making it.

- When this dialogue has been constructive, both the client and the therapist emerge from the rupture with increased understanding and renewed enthusiasm about therapy. In particular, the therapist should resolve to change elements of their practice as a result of client feedback.

Feedback-informed treatment

One way in which therapists can monitor the working alliance from the client perspective is to employ insights from 'feedback-informed treatment' (FIT). This refers to therapy that is based on the therapist seeking ongoing feedback from the client about outcome and process. Brattland, Koksvik, Burkeland, Klöckner, Lara-Cabrera, Miller, Wampold, Ryum and Iversen (2019) conducted a study on FIT and discovered that the strength of the working alliance increased over the course of therapy when therapists used the 'Outcome Rating Scale' (ORS) and the 'Session Rating Scale' (SRS) compared to when they did not. The strengthened alliances led to improved outcomes for clients in this study.

The ORS is a four-item measure[2] designed to assess how well a person is doing a) individually (personal well-being), b) interpersonally (family, close relationships), c) socially (work, school, friendships) and d) overall (general sense of well-being).

The SRS is a measure[3] which is designed to assess the client's experience of the session that they have just had on four items[4] which approximate to three components of the working alliance: a) Relationship (Bonds) ['I did not feel understood, heard and respected' – 'I felt heard, understood and respected']; b) Goals and Topics (Goals) ['We did not work on and talk about what I wanted to work on and talk about' – 'We worked on and talked about what I wanted to work on and talk about']; c) Approach or Method (Tasks) ['The therapist's approach is not a good fit for me' – 'The therapist's approach is a good fit for me']; d) Overall ['There was something missing in the session today' – 'Overall, today's session was right for me'].

In my view, one does not have to buy into the FIT method in order to incorporate such feedback into one's therapy approach, although some therapists (and clients) do appreciate the structure that these two forms give. In particular, regular use of the SRS does help the therapist to identify early markers of an alliance rupture and encourages both therapist and client to discuss these in the reflection process and then to deal with them before they become a full-blown rupture.

Conclusion

Of all the ideas that I discuss in this book, I would say that Bordin's working alliance model has been one of the two most influential on my therapeutic thinking and practice. The second of these two ideas – the role of attitudes in psychological disturbance and health – I will discuss in the next chapter.

Notes

1   It has been found that, of people who only attend one session of therapy, 70–80% found that session helpful given their circumstances (Hoyt & Talmon, 2014). This, of course, means that 20–30% did not find the session helpful and it is my view that, of this group, a number did not return because they did not feel safe in the relationship.
2   The four dimensions of functioning in the ORS are presented as four visual analogue scales which are lines ten centimetres in length. The client is asked to place a mark on each line that corresponds with their experience in the past week.
3   In the SRS, four dimensions of the client's experience of the session are again presented as four visual analogue scales which are lines ten centimetres in length. The client is asked to place a mark on each line that corresponds with their experience of the session in each of the four components.
4   I will present the end points of each of the four dimensions.

Chapter 2

The role of attitudes in psychological disturbance and health

Overview

In this chapter, I will discuss the important role that attitudes play in psychologically disturbed and psychologically healthy responses to life's adversities. First, I will outline why I use the term 'attitudes', rather than the more commonly used term 'beliefs', when discussing what I consider to be the core cognitive feature of psychological disturbance and health. Second, I will explain why I prefer the terms 'rigid and extreme' and 'flexible and non-extreme' to the terms 'irrational' and 'rational' when describing the attitudes that underpin such disturbance and health, respectively. Then, I will distinguish between flexible and non-extreme attitudes and rigid and extreme attitudes, pointing out that both share a common idea and that clients have a choice about what to do after acknowledging this common idea.

Introduction

Every therapist has views about psychological disturbance and health that they bring to their work in therapy. Some therapists may overtly share these views with clients, while others are informed by these ideas without being explicit about them. I remember seeing

DOI: 10.4324/9781003195443-2

a psychoanalytically oriented psychotherapist as a client while doing my counsellor training in the mid-1970s and asking him what concepts he used to understand my problems. Needless to say, he did not tell me. Rather, he interpreted my wish to know. This experience taught me to share such ideas with clients if they wish to know, unless I have a good reason not to.

I mentioned my counsellor training above. I was trained at the University of Aston on a one year full-time diploma course in counselling in educational settings. The course was firmly based on client-centred therapy,[1] and we had a good grounding in its ideas about psychological disturbance and health. However, while its ideas about ego-related problems resonated with me, where the person's problems related to self concerned conditions of worth, I was disappointed that it seemed to have little to say about non-ego problems, where the person's problems concerned their difficulties with bearing discomfort. The practice of client-centred therapy also did not resonate with me.

After the Aston course, I undertook an exploration of other approaches to therapy to see if I could find one that resonated with me. I found the theory and practice of Rational Emotive Behaviour Therapy (REBT)[2] most appealing to me, so I decided to undertake training in it. In retrospect, the reason I was attracted to REBT was its view of psychological disturbance and health as well as its active-directive mode of practice. In this chapter, I will concentrate on the former.

From beliefs to attitudes

REBT has an *ABC* model of psychological disturbance and health. Traditionally, the components of the *ABC* model are described as follows. *A* stands for 'Activating event', *B* stands for the person's 'Beliefs' about the activating event, and *C* stands for the 'Consequences' that the person experiences as a result of the beliefs they hold about the activating event. Originally, REBT was known as Rational Therapy (RT). The founder of RT, Dr Albert Ellis (1958), named the approach Rational Therapy in 1956 because he wanted to emphasise its rational or cognitive features in order to distinguish it from the existing approaches of that time, the main features of which were largely non-cognitive.

Ellis was influenced by philosophers as well as by psychologists (Dryden, 2014). In terms of his theory of psychological disturbance and health, he was perhaps most influenced by Epictetus, the Greek Stoic philosopher. Epictetus' famous statement that 'Men are disturbed not by things, but by the view which they take of them' became the foundation of Ellis's (1958) cognitive model of psychological disturbance. As we have seen from his *ABC* model, Ellis was most interested in the role of what he called 'beliefs' in psychological disturbance and health. Although he rarely defined the term 'beliefs', they can be seen as cognitive appraisals that a person makes about an activating event at *A*, and the type of appraisals that the person makes has a marked effect on their subsequent emotions, behaviours and thinking.

However, I have never been completely happy with the term 'beliefs' when thinking about the mediating factors between *A* and *C*. While there are problems with the term 'belief', it has been retained in part because it begins with the letter *B* and thus shows in REBT's *ABC* framework that adversities at *A* have their impact on a range of psychological responses to these adversities largely because of the 'beliefs' that people hold at *B*.

A number of years ago, I carried out research on how REBT's *ABC* framework is understood by different professional and lay groups.[3] This research revealed a range of confusions and errors made by these groups about each element in the framework (Dryden, 2013). Such confusions and errors about *B* may be cleared up by using the term 'attitude' rather than belief, since the term 'belief' is often used by people in a way that is very different from the way it is used in REBT.

The term 'belief' has been defined by the *Oxford Dictionary of Psychology* (fourth edition, Colman, 2015) as 'any proposition that is accepted as true on the basis of inconclusive evidence'. Thus, a client may say something like 'I believe my boss criticised me' and while they think that they have articulated a belief, this is not actually a belief as the term has been used in REBT, but rather an inference. It is very important to distinguish between an inference at A and an attitude (or belief in the REBT sense) at B and anything that helps this distinction to be made routinely is to be welcomed. Using the term 'attitude' rather than 'belief' in REBT is one way of doing so.

Definitions of the term 'attitude' are closer to the meaning that REBT theorists ascribe to the term 'belief'. Here are three such definitions of the term 'attitude':

- 'an enduring pattern of evaluative responses towards a person, object, or issue' (Colman, 2015);
- 'a relatively enduring organisation of beliefs, feelings, and behavioral tendencies towards socially significant objects, groups, events or symbols' (Hogg & Vaughan, 2005: 150);
- 'a psychological tendency that is expressed by evaluating a particular entity with some degree of favor or disfavor' (Eagly & Chaiken, 1993: 1).

Before deciding to change the term 'belief' to the term 'attitude' in my writings and clinical work, I used the term 'attitude' rather than 'belief' with my clients and found that it was easier for me to convey the meaning of B when I used 'attitude' than when I used 'belief', and they, in general, found 'attitude' easier to understand in this context than 'belief'.

Consequently, I decided to use the term 'attitude'[4] instead of the term 'belief' to denote an evaluative stance taken by a person towards an adversity at A which has emotional, behavioural and thinking consequences (Dryden, 2016). In deciding to use the term 'attitude' rather than the term 'belief', I recognise that when it comes to explaining what the *B* stands for in the *ABC* framework, the term 'attitude' is problematic because it begins with the letter *A*. Rather than use an 'AAC' framework which is not nearly as catchy or as memorable as the *ABC* framework, I suggested using the phrase 'Basic attitudes'[5] when formally describing *B* in the *ABC* framework. While not ideal, this term includes 'attitudes' and indicates that they are central or basic and that they lie at the base of a person's responses to an adversity.

In using the term 'basic', I have thus preserved the letter *B* so that the well-known *ABC* framework can continue to be used. However, when not formally describing the *ABC* framework, I will employ the word 'attitude' rather than the phrase 'basic attitude' when referring to the particular kind of cognitive processing that REBT argues mediates between an adversity and the person's responses to that negative event.

From 'irrational'/'rational' beliefs to rigid and extreme/flexible and non-extreme attitudes

Another change that I initiated is the movement away from the terms 'irrational' and 'rational' to the terms 'rigid and extreme' and 'flexible and non-extreme' when describing the attitudes that underpin psychological disturbance and psychological health. The reason I made that change is that the terms 'irrational' and 'rational' tend to be a turn-off to both clients and non-REB therapists. Towards the end of his career, Ellis himself regretted that he had chosen the name Rational Therapy to describe his therapy. He said that he wished he had called it Cognitive Therapy but didn't do so because the term 'cognitive' was not in vogue in the mid-1950s.[6]

On the other hand, clients can see readily that the attitudes that underpin their psychologically disturbed responses to adversities are rigid and extreme. These terms are less pejorative than the term 'irrational', which tends to be equated in many clients' minds with the term 'crazy' or 'bizarre'. Far from being seen as something to strive for, the term 'rational' is seen by clients as being robot-like and unemotional. On the other hand, the terms 'flexible' and 'non-extreme' when describing the attitudes that underpin psychologically healthy responses to adversities at *A* are more acceptable to clients.

Four types of disturbance-related and health-related attitudes

REBT theory[7] holds that there are four disturbance-related attitudes and four health-related attitudes. In discussing these attitudes, I will deal with each disturbance-related attitude with its health-related counterpart. In taking this tack, I hope to make clear what the differences are between these disturbance-related and health-related attitudes.

Before I do so, let me make the point that, for most of his career, Ellis (e.g. 1983) made the point that rigid attitudes are at the very core of psychologically disturbed responses to adversities and that three extreme attitudes (awfulising attitudes, unbearability attitudes and devaluation attitudes) stem from these rigid attitudes. Conversely, he argued that flexible attitudes are at the very core of psychologically healthy responses to the same adversities and that three non-extreme attitudes (non-awfulising attitudes, bearability attitudes and acceptance attitudes) stem from these flexible attitudes.

Flexible attitudes vs rigid attitudes

The reason REBT's theory of psychological disturbance and health resonated with me was its emphasis on rigid and flexible attitudes being at the core of these states. The way I see it is this. As humans we have desires. We want certain things to happen and other things not to happen. This is a fact about human beings. We are evaluative creatures. While we can adopt a non-evaluative stance such as mindfulness, we generally cannot remain in such a state for long. As such, in my view, any theory of psychological disturbance and health needs to feature humans' evaluative nature, and REBT's standpoint on this issue does just that.

While we have preferences, we also have a choice about what to do with these preferences. We can keep them flexible or make them rigid. So, for example, let's assume that a client wants to do well at a task. The client can choose to keep this preference flexible by negating their demand, 'I want to do well at the task, but I don't have to do so', or to make it rigid by asserting their demand, 'I want to do well, and therefore I have to do so'. Figure 2.1 summarises this.

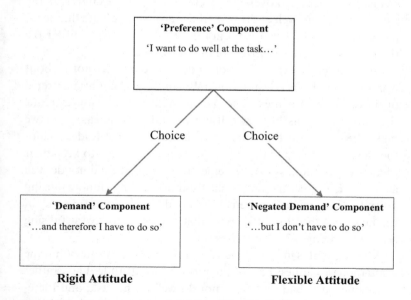

Figure 2.1   **Components of rigid and flexible attitudes**

When a client is in a disturbed frame of mind, they often omit the preference part of their rigid attitude. Thus, rather than state, 'I want to do well at the task, and therefore I have to do so', they will say, 'I have to do well at the task'. Reminding them of the preference component of their rigid attitude helps them to see that they have the choice that I mentioned above, i.e. to keep the preference flexible or to make it rigid.

Non-awfulising attitudes vs awfulising attitudes

When a client's preference is not met, this is known as an 'adversity' in REBT theory. As I mentioned earlier, humans are evaluative in nature and are therefore going to evaluate adversities negatively. The stronger their preference, the more negative will be their evaluations of these adversities. Returning to our example, if the client does not do well at the task, then they will evaluate this negatively (e.g. 'It is bad that I did not do well at the task'). In REBT theory this is known as an 'evaluation of badness'.

While we make evaluations of badness, we have a choice about what to do with these evaluations. We can keep them non-extreme or we can make them extreme. When we keep them non-extreme, they are known as 'non-awfulising attitudes', whereas when we make them extreme, they are known as 'awfulising attitudes'. Thus, the client who failed to do well at the task can choose to keep their evaluation of badness non-extreme, 'It is bad that I did not do well at the task, but it isn't awful that I did not do so' (non-awfulising attitude) or to make it extreme, 'It is bad that I did not do well at the task, and therefore it is awful that I did not do so' (awfulising attitude). Figure 2.2 summarises this.

When a client is in a disturbed frame of mind, they often omit the evaluation of badness part of their awfulising attitude. Thus, rather than state, 'It is bad that I did not do well at the task, and therefore it is awful that I did not do so', they will say, 'It is awful that I did not do well at the task'. Reminding them of the evaluation of

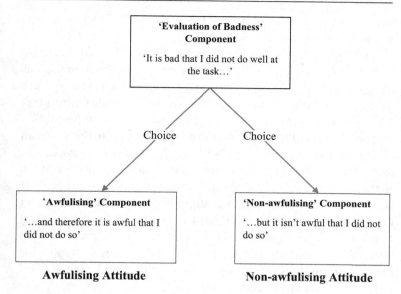

Figure 2.2   Components of awfulising and non-awfulising attitudes

badness component of their awfulising attitude helps them to see that they have the choice that I mentioned above, i.e. to keep the evaluation of badness non-extreme or to make it extreme.

Bearability attitudes vs unbearability attitudes

While non-awfulising attitudes and awfulising attitudes refer to a person's evaluation of how bad the adversity is, bearability attitudes and unbearability attitudes refer to the person's judgement about their capacity to bear the adversity.

When a client faces or thinks about facing an adversity, they will probably think that it will be a struggle for them to bear the discomfort involved in doing so. Returning to our example, if the client does not do well at the task, then they judge that they will struggle to bear this adversity (e.g. 'It is a struggle for me to bear not doing well at the task'). In REBT theory this is known as the 'struggle component'.

While we may struggle to bear facing an adversity, we have a choice about what to do next. We can keep the appraisal of struggle non-extreme or we can make it extreme. When we keep struggle non-extreme, these are known as 'bearability attitudes', while when we make it extreme, these are known as 'unbearability attitudes'. Thus, the client who failed to do well at the task can choose to keep their struggle to bear the adversity non-extreme (bearability attitude) or make it extreme (unbearability attitude). If the client held a bearability attitude, it would be as follows: 'It is a struggle for me to bear not doing well at the task, but I can bear it. Furthermore, it is worth it to me to do so, I am willing to do so, and I am going to do so.' However, if the client held an unbearability attitude, it would be as follows: 'It is a struggle for me to bear not doing well at the task, and therefore I can't bear it.' Figure 2.3 summarises this.

When a client is in a disturbed frame of mind, they often omit the struggle part of their unbearability attitude. Thus, rather than state, 'It is a struggle for me to bear not doing well at the task, and therefore I can't bear it', they will say, 'I can't stand it that I did not do well at the task'. Reminding them of the struggle component of their unbearability attitude helps them to see that they have the choice that I mentioned above, i.e. to keep the struggle non-extreme or to make it extreme.

Unconditional acceptance attitudes vs devaluation attitudes

As I have already mentioned several times in this chapter, humans are evaluative in nature. This is particularly in evidence when we evaluate who or what we hold to be responsible for the adversity that we are facing. Thus, if we hold ourselves to be responsible for

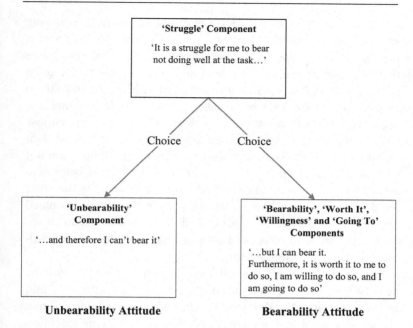

Figure 2.3 **Components of unbearability and bearability attitudes**

the adversity, we will make suitable judgements about ourselves; if we hold another person or persons responsible for the adversity, we will make suitable judgements about them; and if we hold life conditions or the world to be responsible for the adversity, we will judge these accordingly.

When we focus on the aspect of a person (self or other) or of life conditions that we hold responsible for the adversity, we will evaluate this aspect negatively. I call this the 'negatively evaluated aspect' component. Thus, if the client does not do well at the task and they hold themself responsible for this, then they will focus on this aspect and evaluate it negatively (e.g. 'Not doing well at the task is down to me and that is bad').

While we evaluate such aspects negatively, as with non-awfulising and awfulising attitudes, we have a choice about what to do with these evaluations. We can keep them non-extreme or we can make them extreme. When we keep them non-extreme, these are known as 'unconditional acceptance attitudes,'[8] while when we make them extreme, these are known as 'devaluation attitudes'.[9] Thus, the client who failed to do well due to their lack of effort can choose to keep their negatively evaluated aspect non-extreme, thus: 'Not doing well at the task is down to me and that is bad, but I am not worthless for acting badly. Rather, I am a fallible human being who acted badly' (unconditional self-acceptance attitude). On the other hand, the client can choose to make their negatively evaluated aspect extreme, thus: 'Not doing well at the task is down to me and that is bad, and therefore I am worthless' (self-devaluation attitude). Figure 2.4 summarises this.

When a client is in a disturbed frame of mind, they often omit the negatively evaluated aspect part of their devaluation attitude. Thus, rather than state, 'Not doing well at the task is down to me and that is bad, and therefore I am worthless', they will say, 'I am worthless for not doing well at the task'. Reminding them of the negatively evaluated aspect component of their self-devaluation attitude helps them to see that they have the choice that I mentioned above, i.e. to keep the negatively evaluated aspect non-extreme or to make it extreme.

In this chapter, I have focused on the *B* in REBT's *ABC* model – the basic attitudes that underpin both psychologically disturbed and healthy responses to adversity. One important aspect of this idea that makes it so influential for me is that there is a common component in both the rigid/extreme attitude and the flexible/non-extreme attitude pairings and that clients have a choice to keep these shared components flexible/non-extreme or make them rigid/extreme.

In the next chapter, I will show the role that these rigid and extreme attitudes and flexible and non-extreme attitudes play when

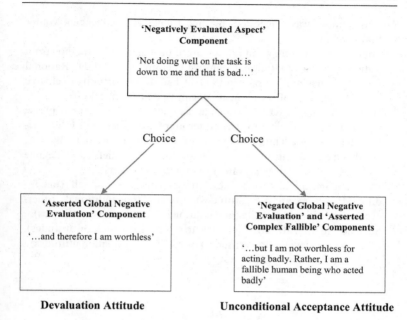

Figure 2.4   Components of devaluation and unconditional acceptance attitudes

placed in context with the adversities at *A* and the aforementioned responses to adversities at *C*.

Notes

1   Now known as person centred therapy.
2   At the time the approach was called Rational-Emotive Therapy.
3   The four groups were: a) authors of textbooks on counselling and psychotherapy; b) REB therapists; c) Albert Ellis (when he was in the twilight of his career) and his wife Debbie Joffe Ellis (2011); and d) patients in a psychiatric hospital who were taught the REBT framework.
4   As this is a new development, please note that other REB therapists (including myself in my previous work) employ the word 'belief'.

5   This phrase was suggested by my friend and colleague Walter Matweychuk.

6   Interestingly enough, when Ellis changed the name of his therapy from Rational Therapy to Rational-Emotive Therapy in 1962 and to Rational Emotive Behaviour Therapy in 1993, he had the opportunity to change the 'rational' part of the name to 'cognitive' but did not do so.

7   When referring to REBT theory and practice in this chapter, please note that I will employ my revised terminology rather than Ellis's original terminology. Thus, I will speak of 'attitudes' rather than 'beliefs', 'rigid and extreme attitudes' rather than 'irrational beliefs', and 'flexible and non-extreme attitudes' rather than 'rational beliefs'.

8   Such unconditional acceptance attitudes can relate to self (unconditional self-acceptance attitudes), others (unconditional other-acceptance attitudes) or life (unconditional life-acceptance attitudes).

9   Such devaluation attitudes can relate to self (self-devaluation attitudes), others (other-devaluation attitudes) or life (life-devaluation attitudes).

Chapter 3

Integrated emotion theory

Overview

In this chapter, I will discuss what I call integrated emotion theory. In doing so, I will look at the early work of Aaron Beck (1976) on the personal domain and inferences made my people in relation to it and the work of Nico Frijda (1993, 1995) in outlining the importance of considering action tendencies and overt behaviour when understanding the emotions for which clients seek help in the face of life's adversities, and what healthy emotional responses are to these adversities. I will also consider the work of Albert Ellis (1983) when discussing what I call the cognitive consequences of holding rigid/extreme attitudes and flexible/non-extreme attitudes in the face of adversities.[1] At the end of the chapter, I will bring together the information I discussed in the previous chapter on attitudes and the information I discuss in this chapter on adversities, actions/action tendencies and subsequent cognitions and feature it all in eight tables of unhealthy negative emotions and their healthy negative counterparts.

DOI: 10.4324/9781003195443-3

The personal domain, inferences and adversities

One of the first books I read on cognitive therapy was *Cognitive Therapy and the Emotional Disorders* by Aaron Beck (1976). One of the concepts in that book that influenced me was Beck's idea of the personal domain. According to Beck, a client's personal domain represents the people, other beings (e.g. animals), objects and ideas that the person holds dear. The closer to the core of the personal domain something is, the more emotionally invested the person is in that 'thing'.[2]

Inferences

An inference is a cognition. It is basically a hunch that a client makes about reality which goes beyond the data at hand. The client's inference may be correct or it may be incorrect, but when the person's emotions are engaged, they tend to think that it is correct and they proceed accordingly.

In therapy, a person's inference in an emotional episode is best understood in relation to their personal domain and the emotions that they experience. For example, when a client is anxious, then they infer that they are facing some kind of threat to their personal domain. I call this an 'adversity' (see below).

However, the reason why I have been an REB therapist for almost all of my professional career as a counselling psychologist is due to its view of psychological disturbance and health. As I showed in the previous chapter, it is the attitudes that a client holds towards the adversity-related inference that determine whether they respond healthily or unhealthily to the inference. In the case of our example, when a person makes a threat-related inference, they will either experience anxiety (what REBT terms an unhealthy negative emotion or UNE) or non-anxious concern (what REBT terms a healthy negative emotion or HNE). When they hold a rigid/extreme attitude towards the threat, they will experience anxiety; when they hold a flexible/non-extreme attitude towards the same threat, they will experience non-anxious concern.

Adversity

As shown above, in an emotional episode a client makes an inference related to their personal domain. In this book, I refer to such an inference as an adversity when the client's emotion is negative. Table 3.1 lists the eight major unhealthy negative emotions for which a client seeks help, their healthy negative counterparts and the adversities that feature in both UNEs and HNEs. I find it useful to have these adversities in mind while assessing the client's emotions and also useful to keep these emotions in mind when assessing the client's adversities.

Dealing with adversities in therapy

There are three main ways of dealing with adversities in therapy: a) to help the client to question their empirical basis, b) to help the client to deal with them whether they occurred or not, and c) to help the client do both. Cognitive therapists would tend to adopt the first strategy, encouraging the client to stand back and consider the empirical status of their adversity-related inference. REB therapists would tend to adopt the second strategy and encourage the client to assume that their adversity-related inference was true before helping them to identify their underlying rigid/extreme attitudes. When a therapist does both, the cognitive therapist would start with the first strategy and move on to the second, while the REB therapist would start with the second and then move on to the first. My own approach would be closer to that of the REB therapist, but to bring the client into the discussion and ultimately go along with what they think will be most helpful to them.

Table 3.1 **Adversity themes associated with unhealthy and healthy negative emotions**

Adversity Themes	Unhealthy/Healthy Negative Emotions
Threat	Anxiety/Concern
Loss/Failure/Undeserved plight experienced by self or others	Depression/Sadness
Breaking a moral code; failing to live up to a moral code; hurting someone	Guilt/Remorse
Falling very short of one's ideal in a social context; others making a negative judgement of one when this happens	Shame/Disappointment
Betrayal or being let down by someone significant when one thinks one does not deserve such treatment; someone significant is not as invested in the relationship as one is oneself	Hurt/Sorrow
Self or other transgresses a personal rule; other threatens self-esteem; frustration	Unhealthy anger/Healthy anger
Threat to valued relationship	Unhealthy jealousy/ Healthy jealousy (concern for one's relationship)
Others have what you value and lack	Unhealthy envy/Healthy envy

Action tendencies and actions

Once a client experiences an emotion, Frijda's (1993, 1995) work shows us that they will tend to act in certain ways. These are known as action tendencies or sometimes as 'urges to act'. REBT's theory of emotions states that when faced with an adversity, a client has the choice to experience an unhealthy negative emotion or a healthy negative emotion. They can actualise that choice by deciding to hold a rigid/extreme attitude or a flexible/non-extreme towards the adversity. If they choose to hold a flexible/non-extreme attitude towards the adversity, then they can help themself to experience the appropriate healthy negative emotion by acting in ways that are consistent with this emotion.

Some clients are not good at distinguishing between healthy negative emotions (HNEs) and unhealthy negative emotions (UNEs) and therefore need help to be able to do so. As it is important for both therapist and client to know whether the client's emotion is a UNE or an HNE, one way that the therapist can help them to make this distinction is by investigating the client's actions or action tendencies. If the client's actions/action tendencies are constructive, then their adversity-related negative emotion is likely to be healthy, and if these are unconstructive, then their negative emotion is likely to be unhealthy.

Choice and action tendencies

The concept of action tendencies is important when it comes to considering therapeutic change. First, it is important to distinguish between an action tendency and an overt action. When a client experiences an action tendency which, if they acted on it, would convert it into an unconstructive action, then it is important for them to appreciate one important point. When they experience the urge to act, they have a choice: to act unconstructively on that urge or to act in an alternative constructive manner. Also, they have a choice again to act unconstructively on their action tendency or to stand back and examine the rigid/extreme attitude that underpins their unconstructive action tendency and then to act constructively in ways that reinforce their flexible/non-extreme attitude. I will discuss in the next chapter the issue of helping clients to stand back from unhealthy psychological processes to enable them to make more informed choices about how to proceed.

Subsequent cognitions

The ABC[3] model of psychological disturbance that is at the heart of Rational Emotive Behaviour Therapy (REBT) is that when people hold rigid and extreme basic attitudes at B towards adversities at A, they will experience a range of disturbed responses at C. These responses are emotional, behavioural and cognitive in nature. Correspondingly, the ABC model of psychological health that is at the heart of REBT is that when people hold flexible and non-extreme basic attitudes at B towards adversities at A, they will experience a range of healthy responses at C. These responses are again emotional, behavioural and cognitive in nature. So far in this chapter, I have considered the emotional and behavioural Cs and in this section I will discuss the cognitive Cs. I call these 'subsequent cognitions' to distinguish them from the cognitions that occur at A[4] and the cognitions that occur at B[5] and to emphasise that they largely stem from the basic attitudes that the client holds towards the adversity. As such, they accompany the emotional and behavioural Cs that I have already discussed.

The nature of the content of subsequent cognitions

Ellis and Dryden (1987) argued that when a client holds an attitude towards an adversity, their subsequent thoughts or cognitions will be influenced by that attitude. When they hold a rigid and extreme attitude towards the adversity, their subsequent thinking about the adversity and related matters will tend to be highly distorted and skewed to the negative. However, when the client holds a flexible and non-extreme attitude towards the same adversity, their subsequent thinking about the adversity and relevant issues tends to be realistic and balanced. In the late 1980s, I carried out a number of studies which supported this point (see Dryden, Ferguson & Clark, 1989; Dryden, Ferguson & Hylton, 1989; Dryden, Ferguson & McTeague, 1989; Bond & Dryden, 1996).

This research suggests that the therapist has an educative role in helping clients understand how they unwittingly construct highly distorted subsequent thinking by holding rigid/extreme attitudes towards adversities. When clients notice their highly distorted thoughts that are skewed to the negative, they need to learn to stand back and distance themselves from these thoughts and do the following:[6]

- Use them to identify and respond to their rigid/extreme attitudes with their flexible/non-extreme attitudinal counterparts.
- Respond to the subsequent thoughts themselves and develop more realistic and balanced thoughts instead.
- Mindfully acknowledge the presence of this subsequent thinking and neither engage with them nor attempt to eliminate them. Rather, act in the same way they would if these thoughts were not present in their mind.

Subsequent cognitive processes

Attitudes also have an effect on subsequent cognitive processes. I will discuss one such process to illustrate this: rumination vs problem-solving.

Rumination vs problem-solving

When a client holds a rigid/extreme attitudes towards an adversity, they will tend to ruminate rather than problem-solve. Nolen-Hoeksema, Wisco and Lyubomirsky (2008: 400) state that 'rumination is a mode of responding to distress that involves repetitively and passively focusing on symptoms of distress and on the possible causes and consequences of these symptoms. Rumination does not lead to active problem solving to change circumstances surrounding these symptoms. Instead, people who are ruminating remain fixated on the problems and on their feelings about them without taking action.' When the client, by contrast, holds a flexible/non-extreme attitude towards the same adversity, they will tend to adopt a problem-solving mindset. They can do that because their flexible/non-extreme attitude frees them from trying to answer unanswerable questions and from being obsessed with their own feelings. Rather than looking backwards and being preoccupied with what they did not do, the client is able to focus on the solvable aspects of their problem and to consider ways of solving it.

Putting it all together

One of my most important contributions to the theory and practice of Rational Emotive Behaviour Therapy has been influenced by the material that I have discussed in this chapter and the previous one and resulted in my bringing all this material together in the form of eight 'emotion tables' (e.g. Dryden, 2012) representing the eight most common emotional problems and their healthy alternatives. Each details the following:

- the unhealthy negative emotion (UNE) vs the healthy negative emotion (HNE) under consideration
- the adversity theme that features in both the UNE and HNE
- the attitudes that underpin the UNE and accompanying behaviour and thinking (rigid/extreme) and that underpin the HNE and accompanying behaviour and thinking (flexible/non-extreme)
- the different behaviours and action tendencies that accompany the UNE (which tend to be unconstructive) and that accompany the HNE (which tend to be constructive)
- the different subsequent thinking that accompanies the UNE (which tends to be highly distorted, skewed to the negative and ruminative) and that accompanies the HNE (which tends to be realistic, balanced and problem-solving).

I present the 'emotion tables' in one master Table 3.2.

Table 3.2 **A guide to the eight emotional problems and their healthy alternatives with adversities, basic attitudes and associated behaviour and thinking**

Anxiety vs concern

Adversity	• You are facing a threat to your personal domain	
Basic Attitude	**RIGID AND EXTREME**	**FLEXIBLE AND NON-EXTREME**
Emotion	Anxiety	Concern
Behaviour/ Action Tendencies	• You avoid the threat • You withdraw physically from the threat • You ward off the threat (e.g. by rituals or superstitious behaviour) • You try to neutralise the threat (e.g. by being nice to people of whom you are afraid) • You distract yourself from the threat by engaging in other activity • You keep checking on the current status of the threat hoping to find that it has disappeared or become benign • You seek reassurance from others that the threat is benign • You seek support from others so that if the threat happens, they will handle it or be there to rescue you • You overprepare in order to minimise the threat happening or so that you are prepared to meet it (NB it is the overpreparation that is the problem here) • You tranquillise your feelings so that you don't think about the threat • You overcompensate for feeling vulnerable by seeking out an even greater threat to prove to yourself that you can cope	• You face up to the threat without using any safety-seeking measures • You take constructive action to deal with the threat • You seek support from others to help you face up to the threat and then take constructive action by yourself rather than rely on them to handle it for you or to be there to rescue you • You prepare to meet the threat but do not overprepare

Subsequent Thinking	*Threat-exaggerated thinking*	
	• You overestimate the probability of the threat occurring • You underestimate your ability to cope with the threat • You ruminate about the threat • You create an even more negative threat in your mind • You magnify the negative consequences of the threat and minimise its positive consequences • You have more task-irrelevant thoughts than in the case of concern	• You are realistic about the probability of the threat occurring • You view the threat realistically • You realistically appraise your ability to cope with the threat • You think about what to do concerning dealing with the threat constructively rather than ruminate about the threat • You have more task-relevant thoughts than in the case of anxiety • You picture yourself dealing with the threat in a realistic way
	Safety-seeking thinking	
	• You withdraw mentally from the threat • You try to persuade yourself that the threat is not imminent and that you are 'imagining' it • You think in ways designed to reassure yourself that the threat is benign or, if not, that its consequences will be insignificant • You distract yourself from the threat, e.g. by focusing on mental scenes of safety and well-being • You overprepare mentally in order to minimise the threat happening or so that you are prepared to meet it (NB once again it is the overpreparation that is the problem here) • You picture yourself dealing with the threat in a masterful way • You overcompensate for your feeling of vulnerability by picturing yourself dealing effectively with an even bigger threat	

Depression vs sadness

Adversity	• **You have experienced a loss from the sociotropic and/or autonomous realms of your personal domain** • **You have experienced failure within the sociotropic and/or autonomous realms of your personal domain** • **You or others have experienced an undeserved plight**	
Basic Attitude	**RIGID AND EXTREME**	**FLEXIBLE AND NON-EXTREME**
Emotion	**Depression**	**Sadness**
Behaviour/ Action Tendencies	• You become overly dependent on and seek to cling to others (particularly in sociotropic depression) • You bemoan your fate or that of others to anyone who will listen (particularly in pity-based depression) • You create an environment consistent with your depressed feelings • You attempt to terminate feelings of depression in self-destructive ways • You either push away attempts to comfort you (in autonomous depression) or use such comfort to reinforce your dependency (in sociotropic depression) or your self- or other-pity (in pity-based depression)	• You seek out reinforcements after a period of mourning (particularly when your inferential theme is loss) • You create an environment inconsistent with depressed feelings • You express your feelings about the loss, failure or undeserved plight and talk in a non-complaining way about these feelings to significant others • You allow yourself to be comforted in a way that helps you to express your feelings of sadness and mourn your loss

| **Subsequent Thinking** | • You see only negative aspects of the loss, failure or undeserved plight
• You think of other losses, failures and undeserved plights that you (and, in the case of the latter, others) have experienced
• You think you are unable to help yourself (helplessness)
• You only see pain and blackness in the future (hopelessness)
• You see yourself being totally dependent on others (in autonomous depression)
• You see yourself as being disconnected from others (in sociotropic depression)
• You see the world as full of undeservedness and unfairness (in plight-based depression)
• You tend to ruminate concerning the source of your depression and its consequences | • You are able to recognise both negative and positive aspects of the loss or failure
• You think you are able to help yourself
• You look to the future with hope |

Guilt vs remorse

Adversity	• You have broken your moral code • You have failed to live up to your moral code • You have hurt someone's feelings	
Basic Attitude	**RIGID AND EXTREME**	**FLEXIBLE AND NON-EXTREME**
Emotion	Guilt	Remorse
Behaviour/ Action Tendencies	• You escape from the unhealthy pain of guilt in self-defeating ways • You beg forgiveness from the person you have wronged • You promise unrealistically that you will not 'sin' again • You punish yourself physically or by deprivation • You defensively disclaim responsibility for wrongdoing • You make excuses for your behaviour • You reject offers of forgiveness	• You face up to the healthy pain that accompanies the realisation that you have sinned • You ask, but do not beg, for forgiveness • You understand the reasons for your wrongdoing and act on your understanding • You atone for the sin by taking a penalty • You make appropriate amends • You do not make excuses for your behaviour or enact other defensive behaviour • You accept offers for forgiveness
Subsequent Thinking	• You conclude that you have definitely committed the sin • You assume more personal responsibility than the situation warrants • You assign far less responsibility to others than is warranted • You dismiss possible mitigating factors for your behaviour • You only see your behaviour in a guilt-related context and fail to put it into an overall context • You think that you will receive retribution	• You take into account all relevant data when judging whether or not you have 'sinned' • You assume an appropriate level of personal responsibility • You assign an appropriate level of responsibility to others • You take into account mitigating factors • You put your behaviour into overall context • You think you may be penalised rather than receive retribution

Shame vs disappointment

Adversity	• Something highly negative has been revealed about you (or about a group with whom you identify) by yourself or by others • You have acted in a way that falls very short of your ideal • Others look down on or shun you (or a group with whom you identify) or you think that they do	
Basic Attitude	RIGID AND EXTREME	FLEXIBLE AND NON-EXTREME
Emotion	Shame	Disappointment
Behaviour/ Action Tendencies	• You remove yourself from the 'gaze' of others • You isolate yourself from others • You save face by attacking other(s) who have 'shamed' you • You defend your threatened self-esteem in self-defeating ways • You ignore attempts by others to restore social equilibrium	• You continue to participate actively in social interaction • You respond positively to attempts of others to restore social equilibrium
Subsequent Thinking	• You overestimate the negativity of the information revealed • You overestimate the likelihood that the judging group will notice or be interested in the information • You overestimate the degree of disapproval you (or your reference group) will receive • You overestimate how long any disapproval will last	• You see the information revealed in a compassionate self-accepting context • You are realistic about the likelihood that the judging group will notice or be interested in the information revealed • You are realistic about the degree of disapproval self (or reference group) will receive • You are realistic about how long any disapproval will last

Hurt vs sorrow

Adversity	• Others treat you badly (and you think you do not deserve such treatment) • You think that the other person has devalued your relationship (i.e. someone indicates that their relationship with you is less important to them than the relationship is to you)	
Basic Attitude	**RIGID AND EXTREME**	**FLEXIBLE AND NON-EXTREME**
Emotion	**Hurt**	**Sorrow**
Behaviour/ Action Tendencies	• You stop communicating with the other person • You sulk and make obvious you feel hurt without disclosing details of the matter • You indirectly criticise or punish the other person for their offence • You tell others how badly you have been treated, but don't take any responsibility for any contribution you may have made to this	• You communicate your feelings to the other directly • You request that the other person acts in a fairer manner towards you • You discuss the situation with others in a balanced way, focusing on the way you have been treated and taking responsibility for any contribution you may have made to this
Subsequent Thinking	• You overestimate the unfairness of the other person's behaviour • You think that the other person does not care for you or is indifferent to you • You see yourself as alone, uncared for or misunderstood • You tend to think of past 'hurts' • You think that the other person has to make the first move to you and you dismiss the possibility of making the first move towards that person	• You are realistic about the degree of unfairness in the other person's behaviour • You think that the other person has acted badly rather than as demonstrating lack of caring or indifference • You see yourself as being in a poor situation, but still connected to, cared for by and understood by others not directly involved in the situation • If you think of past 'hurts', you do so with less frequency and less intensity than when you now feel hurt • You are open to the idea of making the first move towards the other person

Unhealthy anger vs healthy anger

Adversity	• You think that you have been frustrated in some way or your movement towards an important goal has been obstructed in some way • Someone has treated you badly • Someone has transgressed one of your personal rules • You have transgressed one of your own personal rules • Someone or something has threatened your self-esteem or disrespected you	
Basic Attitude	**RIGID AND EXTREME**	**FLEXIBLE AND NON-EXTREME**
Emotion	**Unhealthy anger**	**Healthy anger**
Behaviour/ Action Tendencies	• You attack the other(s) physically • You attack the other(s) verbally • You attack the other(s) passive-aggressively • You displace the attack on to another person, animal or object • You withdraw aggressively • You recruit allies against the other(s)	• You assert yourself with the other(s) • You request, but do not demand, behavioural change from the other(s) • You leave an unsatisfactory situation non-aggressively after taking steps to deal with it
Subsequent Thinking	• You overestimate the extent to which the other(s) acted deliberately • You see malicious intent in the motives of the other(s) • You see yourself as definitely right and the other(s) as definitely wrong • You are unable to see the point of view of the other(s) • You plot to exact revenge • You ruminate about the other's behaviour and imagine coming out on top	• You think that the other(s) may have acted deliberately, but you also recognise that this may not have been the case • You are able to see the point of view of the other(s) • You have fleeting, rather than sustained, thoughts to exact revenge • You think that other(s) may have had malicious intent in their motives, but you also recognise that this may not have been the case • You think that you are probably rather than definitely right and the other(s) as probably rather than definitely wrong

Unhealthy jealousy vs healthy jealousy (or relationship concern)

Adversity	• A threat is posed to your relationship with your partner by a third person • A threat is posed by uncertainty you face concerning your partner's whereabouts, behaviour or thinking in the context of the first threat	
Basic Attitude	**RIGID AND EXTREME**	**FLEXIBLE AND NON-EXTREME**
Emotion	**Unhealthy jealousy**	**Healthy jealousy (relationship concern)**
Behaviour/ Action Tendencies	• You seek constant reassurance that you are loved • You monitor the actions and feelings of your partner • You search for evidence that your partner is involved with someone else • You attempt to restrict the movements or activities of your partner • You set tests which your partner has to pass • You retaliate for your partner's presumed infidelity • You sulk	• You allow your partner to initiate expressing love for you without prompting them or seeking reassurance once they have done so • You allow your partner freedom without monitoring their feelings, actions and whereabouts • You allow your partner to show natural interest in members of the opposite sex without setting tests • You communicate your concern for your relationship in an open and non-blaming manner

Subsequent Thinking	• You exaggerate any threat to your relationship that does exist	• You tend not to exaggerate any threat to your relationship that does exist
	• You think the loss of your relationship is imminent	• You do not misconstrue ordinary conversations between your partner and other men/women
	• You misconstrue your partner's ordinary conversations with relevant others as having romantic or sexual connotations	• You do not construct visual images of your partner's infidelity
	• You construct visual images of your partner's infidelity	• You accept that your partner will find others attractive but you do not see this as a threat
	• If your partner admits to finding another person attractive, you think that they find that person more attractive than you and that they will leave you for this other person	

Unhealthy envy vs healthy envy

Adversity	• Another person possesses and enjoys something desirable that you do not have	
Basic Attitude	**RIGID AND EXTREME**	**FLEXIBLE AND NON-EXTREME**
Emotion	Unhealthy envy	Healthy envy
Behaviour/ Action Tendencies	• You disparage verbally the person who has the desired possession to others • You disparage verbally the desired possession to others • If you had the chance, you would take away the desired possession from the other (either so that you will have it or so that the other is deprived of it) • If you had the chance, you would spoil or destroy the desired possession so that the other person does not have it	• You strive to obtain the desired possession if it is truly what you want
Subsequent Thinking	• You tend to denigrate in your mind the value of the desired possession and/or the person who possesses it • You try to convince yourself that you are happy with your possessions (although you are not) • You think about how to acquire the desired possession regardless of its usefulness • You think about how to deprive the other person of the desired possession • You think about how to spoil or destroy the other's desired possession • You think about all the other things the other has that you don't have	• You honestly admit to yourself that you desire the desired possession • You are honest with yourself if you are not happy with your possessions, rather than defensively trying to convince yourself that you are happy with them when you are not • You think about how to obtain the desired possession because you desire it for healthy reasons • You can allow the other person to have and enjoy the desired possession without denigrating that person or the possession • You think about what the other has and lacks and what you have and lack

Notes

1   These are sometimes referred to as 'subsequent cognitions'. They are thoughts and cognitive processes that accompany emotions.
2   I have noticed one thing about me as a psychologist. It is that once I have become personally invested in a therapeutic idea or concept, that investment continues unless something drastic happens for me to give it up. Thus, I have been personally invested in Bordin's working alliance concept since 1979, in Ellis's concept of irrational and rational beliefs since 1977 and in Beck's concept of the personal domain since 1978.
3   Where A stands for an $\underline{A}$dversity, B stands for the $\underline{B}$asic attitudes that the person holds towards the adversity and C stands for the $\underline{C}$onsequences of holding such basic attitudes towards the adversity.
4   'Adversities' are most often inferential in nature and, as I discussed earlier in this chapter, an inference is a cognition.
5   'Basic attitudes' are evaluative cognitions as discussed in Chapter 2.
6   I present them in the order which an REB therapist would tend to use, although I would discuss this order with a client and encourage them to suggest an order that makes most sense to them. Ideally, all three strategies can be used by the client.

Chapter 4

Responsibility

Overview

In this chapter, I will discuss the important concept of responsibility and its relation to psychotherapy. In particular, I will discuss a) responsibility and thinking; b) responsibility, feelings and attitudes; c) responsibility and decision-making; d) responsibility, action tendencies and behaviour; e) responsibility and the consequences of behaviour; and e) responsibility, blame, victimhood and self-blame.

Introduction

For me, the concept of personal responsibility is perhaps one of the most influential ideas in psychotherapy and certainly it is important for clients to take responsibility if they are going to get anything substantial and long-lasting from therapy.

My view is that a client is responsible for matters which are within their control. The prime areas that a client is able to control are those that belong to them as a person: their thoughts, their feelings, their actions, their decisions and their body. They also have *some* influence over the likely consequences of their actions. It is important to point out, and to make this clear to a client, that they are not in perfect control of any of the above.

DOI: 10.4324/9781003195443-4

Responsibility and thinking

Let me begin by exploring the relationship between responsibility and thinking. From what have become known as the 'white bear' experiments, if a person is invited to think of a white bear and then told to banish these thoughts from their mind, the outcome is usually the opposite of what they have been instructed to do (Wegner, 1989; Wegner & Schneider, 2003).[1]

These experiments show that when a person employs an elimination-based strategy with thoughts, their control over their thoughts tends to be poor. However, if in response to the invitation to banish the thought of a white bear the person employs a mindful, acceptance-based strategy where they notice the presence of the thought relating to the white bear and allow it be there for as long as it is there, then their ability to control the thought increases (Orsillo & Roemer, 2005). Whichever strategy the person employs, they are still responsible for their thinking as these are their thoughts and they have potential, but not perfect, control over them. However, they do need to discover how best to discharge their responsibility.

I mentioned earlier that the 'white bear' experiment involves inviting a client, say, to think of a white bear and then asking them to dismiss such thoughts from their mind. What is the person who issued the initial invitation to the client to think of the white bear and the later instruction to them to dismiss such thinking from their mind responsible for? What that person is responsible for here is their invitation to the client to think of the white bear in the first place and their instruction to them to dismiss the thought in the second place. These actions are within the person's control and thus they are responsible for them. What they are not responsible for is the client thinking or not thinking of the white bear. It is true that their invitation and later instruction may influence the client's thinking but the client, not the interlocutor, is responsible for their own thinking.

Responsibility, feelings and attitudes

In Chapter 2, I discussed the idea that a client's attitude towards an adversity has a decided impact on how they feel and subsequently think about the adversity and how they act in relation to it.

Thus, a client's emotions largely depend on their attitudes towards an adversity. Since the client is largely responsible for the attitudes they have towards an adversity, they can be said to assume the major responsibility for the feelings that stem from these attitudes. They do not have total control over their attitudes or their feelings because the adversity has some bearing on the way that they are going to think and feel.

For example, let's suppose that a client enjoys the company of their friends, but their job has taken them abroad where they do not know anybody. The client is facing an adversity. Being in this situation, therefore, has some bearing on the way the client is going to think, given their desire to be with their friends. Since they are facing an adversity, it is unlikely that they will think, 'Good. I'm pleased that I am away from my friends', or, 'It doesn't matter to me one way or the other that I am cut off from the people I care about'. Indeed, it would be unhealthy for them to think in such ways. However, facing this adversity does not deprive the client of their responsibility altogether for the way they think about their plight. They will have a choice between holding a flexible/non-extreme attitude ('I would prefer to be with my friends, but I don't have to be with them. Not being with them is a struggle but I can stand it.') and holding a rigid/extreme attitude (e.g. 'I would prefer to be with my friends and therefore I have to be with them. Not being with them is a struggle which I can't stand.').

The events that a client faces, particularly adversities, do restrict their choice of what attitudes to take towards such negative events, but they rarely *cause* the attitudes the client adopts. They almost always have a choice of holding flexible/non-extreme attitudes and holding rigid/extreme attitudes and thus almost always have a choice of experiencing a healthy negative emotion (HNE) or an unhealthy negative emotion (UNE). In this way, they are responsible for their attitudes and for the feelings that stem from these attitudes.

Addressing the 'it made me feel' position

One of the tasks of the therapist is to address a common misconception held by many clients that their feelings are caused by the negative events in their lives.[2] In REBT we refer to this as $A–C$ thinking (where A stands for adversity and C, in this case, stands for emotions). The task for the REB therapist in such an instance is clear; they need to help the client gain what may be referred to as 'emotional responsibility' or $B–C$ thinking (where B stands for basic attitudes and once again C stands for emotions). However, most other therapists will want to do something similar even if they may use different terminology.

This task becomes harder for the therapist the more negative the adversity is that the client is facing. Here, the therapist's task is to help the client to see that the adversity contributes to their feelings, but their basic attitude is still the prime determinant. As my late colleague Paul Hauck (1980) once said, A accounts for from 1% to 49% of a person's emotional response to an adversity, while B accounts for from 51% to 99%. In helping the client to see this, it is important for the therapist to do so with kindness and compassion.

Responsibility and decision-making

A client is also largely responsible for the decisions they make in life, even though they may not have all the information they need when they make a decision. Let's suppose that a client has been offered two jobs. They are unemployed and are faced with making three choices. First, they could take job A. Second, they could take job B. Or, third, they could choose to remain unemployed and wait for a better job to come along. In taking this final option, they are, of course, taking the risk that they will not find a better job.

It is the client's responsibility to find out as much as they can about the two jobs that they have been offered and also about the chances of finding a better job if they decide not to take either of them. Let's suppose that the client decides to take job A. It quickly transpires, however, that important information was withheld from them which, if they had known about it, would have meant that they would have made a different decision. The client is still responsible for making the decision that they took, but they are not responsible for the fact that important information was withheld from them. It would be counter-productive, therefore, for the client to demand that they absolutely should have known this information when the reality was that they didn't know it.

This is an important point: the client is not responsible for knowing what they did not know. While the client cannot be held responsible for something that they did not know at a given moment, they are responsible for learning from this experience. Thus, next time they could ask certain questions about a job that they did not ask about job A.

Responsibility, behaviour and action tendencies

When a client takes action, it is clear that as they are the author of their behaviour they can be said to be responsible for it. However, the situation is a little more complicated when it comes to their urges to act or action tendencies.

As I explained in Chapter 3, an action tendency is associated with an emotion. Thus, if a client experiences anxiety, they will tend to withdraw from a threat; when they experience concern, they will tend to approach and deal with the threat. Earlier in this chapter, I argued that the client needs to take responsibility for their feelings about an adversity by recognising that they create these feelings largely by the attitudes that they take towards the adversity. As such, their emotional responsibility comes about through their attitudinal responsibility.

The same is true when considering action tendencies. The client is responsible for creating their action tendencies through their attitudinal responsibility. Thus, their tendency to act towards an adversity at C is largely determined by the basic attitude that they take towards the adversity. Their attitudinal responsibility refers to the fact that they have a choice between taking a flexible/non-extreme attitude or a rigid/extreme attitude towards the adversity. Once the client has experienced an action tendency, they are responsible for whether they act on it or not.

To recap, clients are responsible for creating their action tendencies with respect to adversities through the attitudes they adopt towards these adversities and for which they are responsible (attitudinal responsibility). Having created these tendencies, they are responsible for whether they act on them or not. If they do act on these tendencies, then they are responsible for these behaviours (behavioural responsibility).

Responsibility and the consequences of behaviour

A client also has some responsibility for the likely consequences of their actions. Let's suppose that a client has promised to do a favour for a friend. However, when the time comes for the favour to be done, something more interesting crops up for the client and they decide not to keep their promise. Given the circumstances, it is very likely that the client's friend is going to be disappointed that the client did not keep their promise to do the favour. Here, it can be said that the client is responsible not only for deciding to do something else rather than keeping their promise to their friend (behavioural responsibility) but also for the disappointment of their friend.

However, if the client's friend responds to the broken promise with severe depression, the client cannot be held responsible for their friend's depressed feelings, since these depressed feelings stem largely from the rigid and extreme attitudes the friend holds towards the broken promise.

Responsibility, blame, victimhood and self-blame

What all this means is that it is very important for the client to take responsibility for their thoughts/attitudes, feelings, decisions, actions and the likely consequences of these actions. Unless they assume personal responsibility, they will not strive to change what they can change; rather, they will tend to blame other people or life events for the way they think, feel, act and the decisions that they make. Blaming other people and external events for what the client is really responsible for is a hallmark of poor mental health.

When the client does this, they tend to see themself as a victim and take an 'I am helpless' view towards life. Refusing to accept personal responsibility means that the client also refuses to take control of their life. As such, they look towards others to rescue them and become overly dependent on them. Being a victim, they will tend to complain bitterly about their lot and how unfairly they have been treated by others and by the world.

If the client does this, they will tend to blame their past and their parents for the way they think, feel and act today. Unfortunately, some schools of psychology tend to reinforce this by not distinguishing between past events *contributing* to the way the client thinks, feels and acts today and those same events *causing* the client's thoughts, feelings and behaviour. My view is that a client's past certainly has an influence on their present, but it can rarely be said to cause the way the client responds to life events now. As we have seen, the way they respond now depends largely upon the attitudes they hold towards current and future events. The client may have learned from their parents, for example, that if they fail to do well in life, this means that they are a failure. However, don't forget that in all probability the client has spent many years keeping this attitude alive in their head. My view is that the client is responsible for choosing to keep this attitude alive and that they can learn to change this attitude.

As shown above, it is very important to distinguish between responsibility and blame. While I am arguing that people are responsible largely for the way they think, feel and act, it does not therefore follow that they need to be blamed for their thoughts, feelings and actions, and the consequences of their decisions and actions. Blame involves the philosophy that human beings are bad people if they do bad things and they need to be punished for so doing. In Chapter 2, I argued that people are fallible human beings, neither good nor bad: when they do something bad, they need to take responsibility for it, but they do not have to blame themself for their wrongdoings. When the client blames themself, it tends to stop them from learning from their errors, for if the client deserves to be blamed (by themself and/or by others), this means that they are a bad person, and if the client is a bad person, they will continue to do bad things.

Summary

To summarise, it is important for the client to take responsibility for that which is within their control. Taking responsibility for their thoughts, attitudes, feelings and actions will encourage them to change their rigid and extreme attitudes which underpin their unhealthy negative emotions and self-defeating behaviours. Failure to take such responsibility, on the other hand, means that the client will tend to maintain their rigid/extreme attitudes, which will result in the perpetuation of their emotional problems.

Assuming responsibility for their thoughts, attitudes, feelings, action tendencies and behaviour will help the client to see clearly the options to change and to remain the same, and that they can choose the former rather than the latter. This is the topic of the following chapter.

Notes

1 'Try to pose for yourself this task: not to think of a polar bear, and you will see that the cursed thing will come to mind every minute.' (Fyodor Dostoevsky, *Winter notes on summer impressions*, an essay published in 1863).
2 Referred to as 'adversities' in this book.

Chapter 5

Choice and the power of the second and subsequent responses in the change process

Overview

In this chapter, I will discuss a number of ideas that I have found influential in understanding how people can realistically change in psychotherapy. I will begin by discussing the fact that clients have an experiencing self where their responses to adversities reside and an observing self where they can identify and reflect on the responses of the experiencing self. Then, I will discuss the concepts of choice and options and show what clients need to do to deal with problems which are based on moving away from adversities and disturbed responses to these adversities and with problems which are based on moving towards desired 'objects' that are not good for them. I then discuss the concept of 'standing back' from the disturbed experiences of the experiencing self and how the therapist can help clients to stand back from these experiences and access their observing self. I conclude the chapter by discussing what I call the 'power of the second and subsequent response'.

Introduction

I remember seeing a number of Hollywood movies about psycho-therapy where the 'patient' has a problem and the therapist works with them to achieve a cathartic insight into the origins of the

DOI: 10.4324/9781003195443-5

problem and, hey presto, the problem is resolved. A good example of this is *The Three Faces of Eve*. As Gabbard (2001: 366) notes, 'over and over again audiences have been exposed to patients' being cured after they have de-repressed a traumatic memory and gone through a highly emotional abreaction with the aid of a sympathetic therapist'. As Gabbard emphasises, while this has little resemblance to what happens in the real world of therapy, it has put forward a viewpoint of therapeutic change as being painful for the client, but one that leads to an immediate benefit for the client once the painful experience has been borne.

In this chapter, I will put forward a very different view of the change process, one that I believe is far more realistic than that outlined above.

The experiencing self and the observing self

The idea that psychologically we comprise different parts is one that has been around for many years. For example, Sigmund Freud (1961), the founder of psychoanalysis, distinguished between the 'id', the 'ego' and the 'superego'; Eric Berne (1957), the founder of Transactional Analysis, distinguished between 'Parent', 'Adult' and 'Child' ego states; Albert Ellis (1976), the founder of Rational Emotive Behaviour Therapy, argued that all humans have an 'irrational' part and a 'rational' part of themselves.

In this chapter, I am going to distinguish between the experiencing self and the observing self that I briefly discussed in Chapter 1 (Sterba, 1934). If we, as a species, did not have the capacity to experience and the capacity to observe and reflect on our experience, then psychotherapy would not be possible. Clients differ concerning their facility with these two parts of themselves. Some find it difficult to experience, while others find it difficult to observe their experience. Having said that, in many cases the change process in therapy is based on the capacity of the client to stand back and access their observing self and reflect on the choices that they have when they do so.

Choice

The second influential idea that I want to discuss in this chapter is that of choice. Perhaps one of the most famous quotes in psychology is that by Viktor Frankl (1984: 86) in his book *Man's Search for Meaning*, in which he wrote: 'We who lived in concentration camps can remember the men who walked through the huts comforting others, giving away their last piece of bread. They may have been few in number, but they offer sufficient proof that everything can be taken from a man but one thing: the last of the human freedoms – to choose one's attitude in any given set of circumstances, to choose one's own way.' If a person can exercise choice in such dreadful circumstances as concentration camps, then surely we can exercise choice in more everyday contexts.

Although less well known, the next quote from Frankl (1984: 86–7) follows on directly from that above: 'And there were always choices to make. Every day, every hour, offered the opportunity to make a decision, a decision which determined whether you would or would not submit to those powers which threatened to rob you of your very self, your inner freedom; which determined whether or not you would become the plaything of circumstance, renouncing freedom and dignity to become molded into the form of the typical inmate.'

The reason that I like this second quote, perhaps even more than the first one, is that it stresses the moment-by-moment possibilities that we have for change through the choices that we make moment-by-moment.

Choice and options

When using the term 'choice' with clients, I have learned to be careful since it can easily be misconstrued by them. Thus, when you go to a supermarket to buy a can of beans, you are usually faced with a number of options and need to make a choice among them. The cans are neutral about what you choose and do not exert a pull on you. You may choose a brand because you have tried it before and liked it. On the other hand, you may choose a brand that you have not tried before because you 'feel like' trying something new.

Such a situation is generally not the case in psychological matters. Usually, when a client has a choice to make between two options, for example, in the psychological realm, the person experiences a pull towards something and a pull away from something. Even when the client sees that they have a choice between two options, the reason why change is so difficult is that the client often chooses to go with the grain[1] and selects the option which pulls them towards something that is unhealthy for them. I am going to give two examples of what I mean by this, one where the 'moving towards' option is healthy and the 'moving away from' option is unhealthy and the other where the 'moving away from' option is healthy and the 'moving towards' option is unhealthy.

Scenario 1: 'Moving towards' – healthy – vs 'moving away from' – unhealthy

In this common scenario, a client experiences a disturbed emotion about an adversity and is motivated to move away from the adversity and/or the disturbed emotion in some way. Here are some common 'moving away from' strategies: avoidance, withdrawal, safety-seeking, distraction, using substances to dull the emotional pain, sleeping, reassurance-seeking and checking that a threat does not exist. See Table 3.2 in Chapter 3 for a comprehensive list grouped by emotion.

I want to stress two points here. First, some clients are motivated to move away from the adversity, others from the disturbed emotion and yet others from both. Second, it is important to distinguish between an action tendency and an overt action, as I discussed in Chapter 3. Thus, when a client experiences anxiety about some perceived threat, for example, they may feel an urge to withdraw from the threat and/or from their anxious feelings. At this point they have a choice. Either they can act on the urge and withdraw (which I refer to as 'going with the grain') or they can act against the urge and move towards the threat and the anxious feelings that they will experience. Choosing this option means that the client will need to 'go against the grain' of their urge to withdraw and instead move towards the threat and related anxiety. To do this successfully, the client will first need to bear their feelings of anxiety and develop a flexible and non-extreme attitude towards the threat. Then, they need to choose to implement this 'moving towards' strategy even though the urge to 'move away' is stronger than the option to 'move towards'. I have summarised this in Figure 5.1.

Even if the client acts on the urge and withdraws from the threat and/or the feelings of anxiety that they experience in the face of the threat, they can still choose to stop using their 'moving away from' strategies and begin to use alternative 'moving towards strategies'. Thus, their real problem is not that they act on their urge to withdraw, but that they continue down this pathway. The sooner they recognise that they have implemented a 'moving away from' strategy and choose to stop doing so and to implement a 'moving towards' strategy instead, the better. I have summarised this in Figure 5.2.

Scenario 2: 'Moving away from' – healthy – vs 'moving towards' – unhealthy

In this common scenario, the client experiences an urge to engage in behaviour that is gratifying to them in the short term but is against their longer-term goals. In such cases, their use of 'moving towards' strategies leads them to experience pleasure in the moment and to eliminate the discomfort that they would experience if they used 'moving away' strategies.

I again want to stress two points here. First, some clients are motivated to move towards the desired object because of the pleasure they will experience, others to spare themselves from the

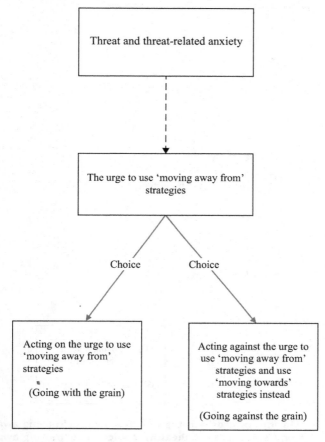

Figure 5.1 **'Moving towards' strategies – healthy – vs 'moving away from' strategies – unhealthy: acting on and against urges**

deprivation discomfort they will experience if they move away from the object or from the disturbed emotion and yet others for both reasons. Second, it is again important to distinguish between an action tendency and an overt action, as mentioned above. Thus, when a client is faced with a desired object that is not good for

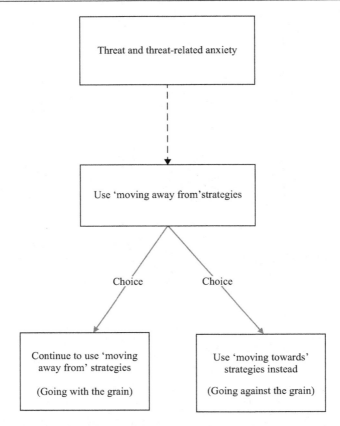

Figure 5.2 **'Moving towards' strategies – healthy – vs 'moving away from' strategies – unhealthy: choice once 'moving away from' strategies have been used**

them (e.g. tasty food that is high in fat and calories), they may feel an urge to experience the pleasure that goes along with eating this food and/or to eliminate the discomfort they would feel if they deprived themself of eating the food. As above, at this point they have a choice. Either they can act on the urge and eat the food (which I refer to as 'going with the grain') or they can act against the urge and move away from the desired object and instead eat bland food that is low in fat and calories. Choosing this option means that the client will need to 'go against the grain' of their urge to eat the unhealthy food. To do this successfully, the client will first need to bear their deprivation discomfort and develop a flexible and non-extreme attitude towards foregoing pleasure. Then, they need to choose to implement this 'moving away from' strategy even though the urge to 'move towards' is stronger than the option to 'move away from'. I have summarised this in Figure 5.3.

Even if the client acts on their urge and moves towards the desired but unhealthy object and the associated pleasure and freedom from deprivation that doing so entails, they can still choose to stop using their 'moving towards' strategies and begin to use alternative 'moving away from' strategies. Thus, their real problem is not that they act on their urge to eat the unhealthy food, but that they continue down this pathway. The sooner they recognise that they have implemented a 'moving towards' strategy and choose to stop doing so and to implement a 'moving away from' strategy instead, the better. I have summarised this in Figure 5.4.

The importance of standing back and accessing the 'observing' self

One of the most important tasks that a client has in psychotherapy is to 'stand back' and reflect on their experience so that they can understand the options available to them and then choose the one that is healthier for them. If the client does not do this, then they are very likely to 'go with the grain' of their unhealthy experience and thus unwittingly maintain their problem (as discussed in the previous section). Standing back does not guarantee that the person will choose the healthiest option available to them, but it does increase the chances that they will do so.

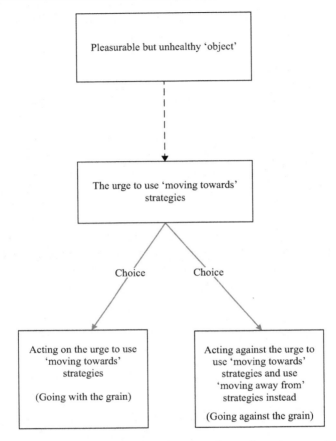

Figure 5.3 **'Moving away from' strategies – healthy – vs 'moving towards' strategies – unhealthy: acting on and against urges**

Standing back in the therapy room

It is important for the therapist and client to be able to stand back and reflect on the work that they have been doing in therapy and the work that they have yet to do. I call this the 'reflection process', which I first discussed in Chapter 1. The way I explain this to clients in therapy is as follows:

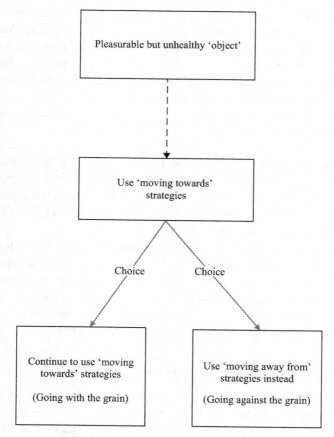

Figure 5.4 'Moving away from' strategies – healthy – vs 'moving towards' strategies – unhealthy: choice once 'moving towards' strategies have been used

Sometimes one or other or both of us may wish to discuss something that has happened or is happening in therapy. To do this, it is important that we stand back from the action, as it were, and reflect together on our experiences of whatever needs to be discussed. When we do this, we are engaging in something that I call the 'reflection process'. I suggest that when either of us wants to discuss something about the process of therapy or what you are getting out of this process, we should feel free to say something like, 'I would like to discuss something in the reflection process'. Once either of us says this, the other should agree to this request and both should stand back and reflect on whatever issue has been flagged for discussion. Does this make sense to you?

The purpose of emphasising the ideas of 'standing back' and 'reflection' here is to encourage both the therapist and client to get into an objective frame of mind where they can discuss whatever needs to be discussed free from the distraction of strong feelings (particularly unhealthy negative feelings).

I used to think that this reflection process, which is a forum for the therapist and client to discuss matters pertaining to the therapy in which they are involved, was 'extra to' or 'outside' therapy. I now see it as an integral part of therapy and a vehicle for demonstrating the state of the relationship with respect to the degree of mutual respect, acceptance and trust present in that relationship.

Standing back outside the therapy room

I think that when the client gets used to using the reflection process in the therapy room to stand back and reflect on their experience, this helps them to do something similar outside the therapy room. The therapist can help the client to do the following:

- To find a physical way to stand back from their experience which makes sense to them.

    This may involve the client literally taking a step back when they are experiencing a disturbed emotion or an urge to act in a self-defeating way. Other ways of standing back might involve the client standing up, changing their body posture, changing their position in some way or moving to a different room. If a client needs to be alone to stand back and reflect, then they can go to the toilet to get privacy. One of my clients who used to smoke, but no longer does so, chose the physical act of taking a puff on an imaginary cigarette as a way of helping her to calm down, stand back and reflect on her experience.

- To stand back by writing down their experience.

  Another common way that people get distance from their painful experiences is by writing them down. The very act of getting something out of one's head onto paper helps the person to stand back from their experiences. This is one of the reasons why thought records are helpful in cognitive behaviour therapy. They help the client to stand back and identify troublesome thoughts, dysfunctional feelings and unconstructive actions or action tendencies. These forms are particularly helpful if the client can use them concurrently when they begin to disturb themself about an adversity which features in their problem. The retrospective use of these forms, while helpful, does not help the client to stand back and observe their experience while they are having it.

- To use mindfulness and relaxation techniques to help the person stand back.

  While mindfulness and relaxation methods are used in psychotherapy for a number of reasons, they can be used by clients to get into a frame of mind where they can then make sense of their experiences, identify their options and select a healthier way forward. Here, such techniques are employed as a means to an end and not as an end in themselves.

Utilising the power of the second and subsequent responses in the change process

When asked what they want to achieve in therapy, clients often nominate the absence of disturbed processes as their therapeutic goal. As discussed in Chapter 1, such goals are unrealistic as it is not possible for anyone to be anxiety free, for example. Rather than eradicate dysfunctional responses, it is important, in my view, that clients recognise that this is not possible. Indeed, if they set absence of unhealthy negative emotions as a goal, and particularly if they are rigid about this, then they will end up by disturbing themselves about their disturbance.

Rather than strive towards such an unrealistic goal, my view is that it is important to encourage a client to see that their initial disturbed response is not their problem. Rather, what is problematic is their choice to take a path which results in them unwittingly perpetuating their disturbance. To counter this tendency, I recommend that the therapist encourages the client to see that when they have begun to disturb themself, which is their first response, they have the option to stand back in some way (see above); this is their second response. They then have the option of responding to that disturbance by dealing with the factors that account for that disturbance, which is their third response. In this way, their second and subsequent responses are more important in the change process than their first response. Once a client has accepted what I call the 'power of the second and subsequent responses', then they can be helped to use the information and methods detailed in this chapter to effect personal change by going against the grain of their disturbed responses to adversity until their healthy responses to the same adversity go with the grain.

Note

1   I use the term 'going with the grain' here to describe a situation where a client chooses an option that is familiar but unhealthy for them.

Chapter 6

Flexibility, pluralism and idiosyncratic practice

Overview

In this chapter, I will argue in favour of the idiosyncratic practice of psychotherapy, and to that end I will discuss the concepts of flexibility and pluralism.

Introduction

One of the fundamental axioms in the field of psychotherapy is the importance of responding to each client as a unique individual. Although the field of psychotherapy is full of good empirically based suggestions for helping people with 'grouped' problems, the therapist has to take these 'findings' and apply them to the unique client in front of them.

If this is true for clients, it is also true for therapists. In my experience, therapists can seek to practise in ways that highlight or minimise their uniqueness as a person. When a therapist chooses to highlight their individuality, they tend to draw on a number of ideas. Here, I will discuss three such ideas: flexibility, pluralism and idiosyncratic practice.

DOI: 10.4324/9781003195443-6

What does it mean to practise an approach rigidly or flexibly?

Every approach to therapy has practical procedural rules that can be interpreted flexibly or rigidly. In this section, I will use the approach to therapy I practise as an example. Thus, in REBT, there is a treatment sequence which suggests to therapists an order in which interventions are to be made (Dryden, DiGiuseppe & Neenan, 2010). When these rules are applied rigidly, an REB therapist would use the recommended sequence even when there was evidence that this sequence was not working. So, rigidity in REBT occurs when therapists stick dogmatically to procedural rules and exclude specific interventions which may be helpful even if they are not generally recommended by the approach.

What then are the markers of flexibility? Let me be clear that I do not equate flexibility in the practice of REBT with being laissez-faire in an 'anything goes' sense. Nor do I mean that all alternative approaches are given equal weight. A therapist who favours particular ways of working is being flexible when they include therapeutic methods in their therapy that they may not favour when it is indicated that it would be beneficial to do so. Thus, therapists who have preferred ways of working (like REBT) but are prepared to make compromises with their preferences are being flexible (Dryden, 1987). Thus, in REBT, the therapist prioritises attitude change as the preferred way of helping people address their problems effectively. However, the flexible REB therapist recognises that while facilitating such attitude change is desirable, there are others ways of helping clients if effecting such attitude change is not possible. These changes are:

- *inferential change* – helping people to change their distorted inferences without effecting attitude change
- *behaviourally based change* – helping people to change their unconstructive behaviour without effecting attitude change

- *changing the environment* – helping people to remove themselves from adversity without effecting attitude change.

Pluralism in psychotherapy

Pluralism can be defined as the philosophical belief that 'any substantial question admits of a variety of plausible but mutually conflicting responses' (Rescher, 1993: 79). More than that, it is an ethical commitment to valuing diversity and a wariness towards monolithic, all-consuming 'truths', because of the way that they can suppress individuality and difference through non-deviation from a singular Truth. In respect to therapy, this pluralistic standpoint implies that there are a variety of views that can be taken on a wide range of therapeutic issues, and that there is no inherent right or wrong way, but obviously some ways will eventually prove to be more helpful than others in solving problems and realising goals. However, just because there is no inherent right or wrong way, this does not mean that unrestrained relativism is being advocated. Responsible or restrained relativism does not shy away when necessary from saying things are right or wrong, true or false, in a strong probabilistic manner. So, the focus in therapy, from this perspective, is on the possible usefulness of what is being proposed from whatever source at any given time. This is not inconsistent with the idea that the therapist can have a preferred approach to therapy, but it points out that the pluralistic REB therapist looks outside of REBT to help clients whenever necessary. In what follows, I will discuss the two pillars of pluralism and a number of pluralistic principles that are based on these two pillars (Cooper & Dryden, 2016).

The two pillars of pluralism

There are two pillars that underpin a pluralistic approach to coaching: a) pluralism across therapeutic orientations and b) pluralism across perspectives.

Pillar 1: Pluralism across therapeutic orientations

This means that a therapist who values pluralism is open to considering a variety of different ways in which clients can be helped to a) address their problems, b) set therapeutic goals, c) work towards achieving these goals, and d) deal with obstacles to the pursuit of these goals. Taking this open-minded stance poses a direct challenge to the narrowing effects of schoolism whereby the therapist stays within the pure confines of a particular theory or set of techniques.

Pillar 2: Pluralism across perspectives

A pluralistic approach to therapy advocates that *both* participants in the therapy relationship – clients as well as therapists – have much to offer when it comes to making decisions concerning therapeutic goals and the selection of therapy tasks and methods. This means that a pluralistic approach emphasises shared decision-making and feedback between clients and therapists. It draws upon the perspectives of both participants.

The principles of pluralism

These two pillars of the pluralistic approach to therapy can be summarised in the following principles:

- There is no one absolute right way of conceptualising clients' problems and goals – different viewpoints are useful for different clients at different points in time.
- There is no one absolute right way of practising therapy – different clients need different things at different points in time and therefore therapists need to have a broad therapy practice repertoire.
- Disputes and disagreements in the therapy field may, in part, be able to be resolved by taking a 'both/and' perspective, rather than an 'either/or' one.

- It is important that therapists respect each other's work and recognise the value that it can have.
- Therapists should ideally acknowledge and celebrate clients' diversity and uniqueness.
- Clients should ideally be involved fully at every stage of the coaching process.
- Clients should ideally be understood in terms of their strengths and resources, as well as their areas of struggle.
- Therapists should ideally have an openness to multiple sources of knowledge on how to practise therapy: including research, personal experience, and theory.
- It is important that therapists take a critical perspective on their own theory and practice, which means being willing to look at their own investment in a particular position and having the ability to stand back from it.

Idiosyncratic practice

One of the phases that therapists tend to go through as they are learning their craft is to copy their teachers or role models. Thus, at the beginning of my career, when I was learning Rational Emotive Behaviour Therapy (REBT), I sounded very much like Albert Ellis doing therapy. However, this is usually a passing phase and it certainly was in my case. I learned the value of doing REBT my way.

Indeed, I discovered that no two REB therapists even approach the same client in the same way. In the summer of 1994, Albert Ellis conducted a single therapy session with a client I called 'Jane'. Very soon after, I was asked to have a single session with 'Jane' on the same issue. Both sessions were recorded, and in 2010 a special issue of the *Journal of Rational-Emotive and Cognitive-Behavior Therapy* was devoted to a comparison of these two sessions. This analysis showed that on the same issue with the same client in a similar time frame the founder of REBT and one of its leading practitioners conducted sessions in a very different way (Dryden, 2010a).

My idiosyncratic practice of REBT

Before the publication of the 'Jane' sessions, I wrote an article detailing what I saw as my idiosyncratic practice of REBT (Dryden, 2001). These are the elements that I discussed in that article:

- developing relationships with clients based on the principle of 'informed allies'
- developing a 'case conceptualisation' with complex 'cases'
- developing an REBT-influenced problem and goals list with clients
- working with specific examples of target problems at the beginning of therapy
- identifying the critical A in the assessment process (i.e. the adversity that features in the client's problem)
- focusing on thinking Cs as well as emotional and behavioural Cs
- helping clients to develop and rehearse the full version of rational beliefs[1]
- encouraging clients to voice their doubts, reservations and objections to REBT concepts and therapeutic process
- deliberately instructing clients in the skills of REBT
- encouraging clients to take responsibility for their change process
- using vivid methods to promote change
- using humour to develop rapport and promote change.

A year after the publication of this article, I edited a book on the idiosyncratic practice of REBT in which a number of REB therapists reflected on their own idiosyncratic practice of this approach to therapy (Dryden, 2002a). This theme of idiosyncratic practice was taken up by Suzanne Keys (2003), who edited a similar book on the idiosyncratic practice of person-centred therapy. It would be interesting to see therapists from other approaches, as well as integrative and pluralistic therapists, reflect on their idiosyncratic practice.

Note

1 I now refer to these as flexible and non-extreme attitudes (see Chapter 2).

Chapter 7

Learning from what therapists do, not from what they say they do

Overview

When I look back over my career as a therapist and reflect on what were the most influential experiences in helping me to develop as a therapist, most of them involved me learning from what people do in therapy rather than from what they say they do. So in this chapter I will review some of these formative experiences and explain why they were so important in fostering my therapeutic thinking and skills. I will begin by discussing a variety of experiences that I had watching therapists practise therapy, listening to them practise therapy and reading transcripts of them practising therapy. Then I will discuss what I have learned from watching and listening to myself practise therapy and from reading my own transcripts of therapy sessions.

Learning from watching, listening to and reading about others practising therapy

Over the years, I have discovered that there is only so much that I can learn from reading books on therapy and engaging in role-plays with peers on a training course. While these activities are useful, I have learned so much more from watching and listening

DOI: 10.4324/9781003195443-7

to therapists practise therapy and from reading and studying transcripts of their unedited sessions.

The 'Gloria Films'

I was originally trained in 'client-centred' therapy,[1] a humanistic approach to therapy founded in the 1940s by Carl Rogers. While the theory that underpinned the therapy resonated with me, I did not experience an easy fit between the way I was being asked to practise and my natural way of being. That became clear to me when we watched Carl Rogers' session with a client known as 'Gloria'.[2] However, on that course, there was no alternative and I bravely persisted in trying to be as client-centred as I could while experiencing growing discomfort. I found the prohibition placed on asking questions particularly difficult.

While Carl Rogers' work with Gloria did not resonate with me, I was more impressed with Albert Ellis's session with her. While far from perfect, I was struck by Ellis's focused work and the questions he asked to elicit important information.

After a brief but unproductive exposure to the theory and practice of psychodynamic therapy, I had the opportunity to attend some training sessions in REBT held in Britain which persuaded me that I wanted to train more fully in this approach. This led me to spend a month at what is now known as the Albert Ellis Institute, where I did two certificated training courses and had the opportunity to serve as Albert Ellis's co-therapist in the groups he ran at his Institute.

Being Albert Ellis's co-therapist in group therapy

Serving as Ellis's co-therapist meant helping him on four evenings a week to run a general, open REBT group. My tasks were to make a note of what clients discussed and particularly the homework assignments that they agreed to do at the end of their 'turn' (see below). Then after 60 minutes the group would go to a different room and work with just the co-therapist, leaving Ellis to see another group or more individual clients.

Ellis basically did individual therapy in a group. He would first work with a client himself and then, when he had completed his work, he would invite group members to offer their contributions. Here, Ellis would reinforce group members' good suggestions and address problematic elements in other contributions. I was struck by how quickly Ellis was able to get to the heart of a client's concern, help them to identify their underlying rigid or extreme attitude and challenge it clearly with a degree of humour. I was also struck by how much practical problem-solving went on in the group. Sometimes there was more of such problem-solving than the more classical REBT work with its attitudinal emphasis.

Right from the start, Ellis encouraged me to intervene as I saw fit during the time when he was the principal group therapist. Once a week during that month I had individual meetings with Ellis where he encouraged me to share my observations on the work that he did in the group and ask him any questions. He also gave me feedback on my own contributions to the group.

This experience helped to shape my approach to running groups which I later wrote about (Dryden, 2002b).

Being David Burns' co-therapist in individual therapy

Three years after my intensive month with Albert Ellis, I spent six months in 1981 learning cognitive therapy at the Center for Cognitive Therapy in Philadelphia under the direction of Aaron Beck. The Center had two or three training videotapes and one of my assignments was to check the accuracy of the transcripts against these videotapes. Once I had done so, I studied the tapes and transcripts closely, trying to work out why the therapists intervened as they did. I will discuss this practice in greater depth below.

While my stay at the Center for Cognitive Therapy was instructional, I benefited more from my experiences serving as co-therapist to Dr David Burns in his individual practice. David Burns had worked closely with the Center, but they went their separate ways after he published his best-selling book *Feeling Good: The New Mood Therapy* (Burns, 1980). I met David soon after beginning my stay at the Center and he invited me to join him as his co-therapist with those patients that he saw before I began my working day at the Center (between 7.30am and 9.00am). David Burns is a very personable man and I learned not only how to use many of the then popular cognitive therapy techniques, but also how to do so in a way that enhanced the working alliance between therapist and client.

As Ellis did, Burns encouraged me to intervene as I saw fit in his individual sessions, and we discussed our work in the weekly meetings we had for this purpose.

Listening to Albert Ellis's therapy tapes

Until recently I have made annual trips to the Albert Ellis Institute, usually to serve on the Institute's faculty on their professional training programmes. One of the experiences I used to benefit from when I was there was listening to audiotapes of Albert Ellis's therapy sessions. Ellis used to record his individual therapy sessions regularly on audiotape and place the cassettes in a box in the Fellows' room so that anyone who was interested could listen to them. I devoured them as it was a great opportunity to learn what Ellis did in his therapy sessions and how he did it. While a prolific writer, Ellis's writings tend to be quite general and it is difficult to learn how to be a good REB therapist from his writings alone, in my opinion. Consequently, these cassette tapes were a godsend to me. Here is a sample of what I learned from listening to Ellis's therapy tapes:

- His approach to sessions was focused, but relaxed.
- In the first session he taught the client the *ABC* model, usually by using the 'Money Model' as a teaching aid (see Appendix).
- He was very focused while disputing a client's rigid/extreme attitude and used Socratic disputing methods until it was clear that they were not effective. In such cases, he switched to being didactic.
- He used a lot of stories, analogies and metaphors to make 'rational points'.
- He generally set a homework assignment and checked it in the following session.
- Ellis offered an hour session and a half-hour session. He would be more time efficient in the 30-minute sessions, often covering the same ground in the 30-minute session as in the 60-minute session.
- He did not use as much humour in his regular therapy sessions as he did in his public demonstration sessions.
- There was more practical problem-solving in his sessions than one might expect from his writings.

The Friday Night Workshop

Albert Ellis ran his Friday Night Workshop every Friday night at his Institute when he was in town from 1965 until 2015. At these workshops, Ellis interviewed two members of the audience who volunteered to discuss an emotional problem for which they needed help. Ellis would interview the volunteer for about 30 minutes and then invite members of the audience to ask questions of him and the volunteer, as well as to make observations on the therapy session. The volunteer would then be given a recording of the session for their later review. Ellis and Joffe (2002) discovered that the vast majority of volunteers found this a helpful experience and most of them also benefited from the audience comments.

Over the years, Ellis's work at his Friday Night Workshop became increasingly formulaic. He normally did the following:

- He asked for a problem at the outset.
- He identified the volunteer's main disturbed emotion.
- He identified the client's main adversity, usually in general terms.
- He identified and disputed the client's rigid attitude. Sometimes, however, he would identify and dispute the client's main extreme attitude, particularly self-devaluation.
- He would usually help the client to construct their alternative flexible attitude (or main non-extreme attitude).
- He used Rational-Emotive Imagery to give the volunteer in-session imaginal practice at disputing their rigid/extreme attitude.
- He then suggested the use of what he called 'operant conditioning'. He would elicit what the volunteer both enjoyed doing (e.g. watching TV) and disliked doing (e.g. the washing up). Then Ellis would urge the volunteer not to watch TV until they had practised REI, and if the client still did not practise it by a specific time, they should do the washing up.
- All this work was done with a liberal sprinkling of humour.

When Ellis was at the height of his powers, his work with volunteers at the Friday Night Workshop was creative, fluent and well-paced. I used to sit there privately doing my own assessment of the client's problem and rehearsing what I would say next and would always learn from Ellis how to get to the heart of the matter in a more efficient way than I would have done.

Studying therapy transcripts

I mentioned earlier in this chapter that when I did a six-month training course at the Center for Cognitive Therapy in Philadelphia, one of my tasks was to check that the training videotapes that they had at that time had been accurately transcribed. After finishing my task, I realised that by studying the transcripts closely I could learn a great deal about how the therapists in these videos practised cognitive therapy. So, I pored over these transcripts and, every time I did, I discovered something new about how to practise cognitive therapy.

Growth through Reason

Although I enjoyed my sabbatical at the Center for Cognitive Therapy, I retained my allegiance to REBT and decided to deepen my own skills in REBT by studying transcripts of REBT sessions that were published in a wonderful book called *Growth through Reason* (Ellis, 1971). In this book, Ellis presents verbatim transcripts of actual therapy sessions and periodically comments on them, including those that he conducted himself. Apart from Ellis's insightful commentary, what was particularly valuable to me was reading how different REB therapists practise in different ways,[3] and I learned how I could incorporate these different ways of working into my own practice of REBT. Again, I found that this book was a treasure trove of insights into how to practise REBT. Every time I read a transcript, I found something instructive that I hadn't appreciated before.

Rational Emotive Behaviour Therapy: Learning from Demonstration Sessions

In the mid-1990s, I established a master's course in Rational Emotive Behaviour Therapy and decided to give the students an option to study up-to-date REBT transcripts in depth, so I published a book entitled *Rational Emotive Behaviour Therapy: Learning from Demonstration Sessions* (Dryden, 1996) which presented one demonstration REBT session conducted by Albert Ellis and one conducted by me, together with my commentary on these sessions.

Albert Ellis Live!

It has been a feature of the way I train therapists that I like to demonstrate my way of working, which I did on my master's programme and which I still do now when I run training courses. However, students asked for more transcripts of Ellis's work so Ellis and I published a book called *Albert Ellis Live!* (Dryden & Ellis, 2003) which presented five of Ellis's best single-session demonstration sessions with my commentary. These sessions showed Ellis at the height of his therapeutic powers and much can be learned from reading and re-reading the transcripts. In the opening chapter of that book, I present what I learned from poring over these verbatim reports.

Two REB therapists and one client

As mentioned in Chapter 6, in the summer of 1994 Albert Ellis and I each had a single session with a woman named 'Jane', which were both recorded. In 2010 a special issue of the *Journal of Rational-Emotive and Cognitive-Behavior Therapy* was devoted to a comparison of these two sessions. Both transcripts were presented and commented upon and conclusions drawn. A review of the sessions shows that Ellis and I approached our sessions differently and it is useful to speculate on the reasons why. Close study of these transcripts can help the student of REBT see that there is no set way of practising REBT, and even leading REB therapists can differ when the same client brings up the same issue in their session (Dryden, 2010a, 2010b).

Learning from doing live demonstrations of therapy

I have always maintained that it is important for therapists to demonstrate how they work when they are running training courses and workshops. I have endeavoured to do this throughout my career and know that this has been appreciated by members of my audience. It is my usual practice both to record the demonstration sessions and to have verbatim transcripts of them made later. I ask the volunteer for permission to do both and will share them with the person on email request.

When I offer to demonstrate my work, I make clear what my conditions are:

- The audience members should indicate that they are prepared to operate on the ethical principle 'What is said here, stays here'.
- I will only work with a person who has a genuine current problem for which they are seeking help. I will not work with a problem that a person used to have but no longer has. I will also not work with a person who is playing the role of someone else (e.g. a client).
- In choosing a problem, the volunteer should only select a problem that they are prepared to discuss in a public setting.
- I ask for complete silence when I am working with the volunteer.
- As mentioned above, I generally record the session for my own use and for the use of the volunteer and ask that nobody else records the session.

This may sound strange, but I do demonstrations of therapy not just to teach my audience; I also do them in order to learn from the experience myself. There are three sources of such learning: a) audience and volunteer feedback; b) listening to recordings of the sessions; c) studying transcripts of the sessions.

Audience feedback

After the volunteer and I have finished our session, I invite the audience to ask questions of the volunteer or myself and to offer feedback. I also get feedback from the volunteer when an audience member asks them to comment on their experience of the session. Sometimes, audience members ask for reasons why I took a particular path in the session and comment that they may have taken a different path. Such questions and comments are useful for me to reflect on how my clinical thinking affected my behaviour (Dryden, 2009) as well as to learn how other people would have approached the session differently. Perhaps the two most frequent questions I and the volunteer are asked are: a) 'What was your experience of the session?' and b) 'How did you feel being asked so many questions?'[4] I have been struck by the near uniformity of the answers given by the volunteer in response. First, they generally say that they were a little nervous at the beginning, usually about speaking about their problem in public, but that this feeling disappeared soon after.[5] Second, the volunteers generally have no problem with my questions.

Listening to recordings of the sessions

Up to the present,[6] I have carried out over 380 demonstration sessions and have recorded all of them. After a reasonable period of time I listen to each recording and review what I liked about my work and what I did not like about it. In doing so, I make a note of how I could have improved my interventions. In doing this I have refined my ability to:

- identify the main adversity that features in the volunteer's problem
- identify the factors that account for the volunteer unwittingly maintaining their problem
- help the volunteer to select the most viable alternative to these maintaining factors
- encourage the volunteer to rehearse this viable alternative
- identify and deal with obstacles to implementing this selected solution.

Studying transcripts of the sessions

As mentioned above, I have a transcript made of every demonstration session that I conduct. While listening to the recording session helps me to determine how I could have improved my work in broad terms, reading the transcript of the session helps me to focus on more specific matters. For example, reading the transcript helps me to reflect about how I could have used different words in making my interventions more effective. It also helps me to consider how I could have expressed myself in simpler terms and in a more economical way.

What I find particularly helpful is listening to a recording while studying the accompanying transcript. In this way, I am able to supervise myself in increasing my therapeutic skills when carrying out demonstration sessions. This work has formed the foundation for my work in single-session therapy, which I will describe in the final chapter of this book.

Notes

1   Now known as person centred therapy.
2   Gloria was interviewed by Rogers, Fritz Perls (the founder of Gestalt Therapy) and Albert Ellis (the founder of Rational Emotive Behaviour Therapy). The interviews were filmed and these films are now referred to as the 'Gloria Films'.
3   I later edited a book to which different REB therapists contributed chapters detailing their idiosyncratic practice of REBT (Dryden, 2002) – see Chapter 6.
4   The term 'so many questions' is of course loaded and reveals the questioner's sceptical attitude towards the use of questions in the session.
5   I deliberately place the volunteer's seat to face me so that they can't see the audience.
6   As of 1 June 2020.

Chapter 8

Single-session therapy

Overview

In this chapter, I discuss single-session therapy (SST), a field whose ideas I have found to be particularly influential in the latter stages of my career. First, I discuss the nature of single-session therapy and its foundations. Next, I consider the concept of 'help provided at the point of need' and discuss the ideas that underpin this mode of responding to requests for help. Following on, I discuss the goals of SST and deal with the most frequently asked question of this mode of service delivery: who is suitable for such help? I then outline at some length the single-session therapy mindset and its impact on SST good practice. Finally, in an afterword, I briefly outline how these ideas have impacted on my broader practice as a therapist.

Introduction

There have been two major strands in my career as a therapy practitioner, trainer and supervisor. The first is as a Rational Emotive Behaviour Therapist. I have practised REBT, albeit flexibly and from a pluralistic perspective (see Chapter 6), since 1978 and it still informs a lot of my work in the field. However, in 2014 I retired

DOI: 10.4324/9781003195443-8

from my full-time post at Goldsmiths University of London and was looking for a new challenge. This resulted in me devoting much of my time to training professionals in single-session therapy (SST) and practising it myself, which represents the second major strand in my career. In the previous chapter, I explained how much I learned from watching and listening to others do therapy and from listening to myself do live demonstrations of therapy. I also discussed how much I have benefited from reading and studying transcripts of single sessions of therapy conducted by others and by myself. This helps to explain why I chose in the latter part of my career to specialise in SST. In this final chapter, then, I will review the ideas that underpin single-session therapy which I have found particularly influential.

The nature of single-session therapy

Single-session therapy (SST) can best be seen as an intentional endeavour where both the therapist and the client set out with the objective of helping the client in one session knowing that more help is available (Hoyt, Bobele, Slive, Young & Talmon, 2018). There are situations where SST is just that – a single session of therapy where there is no possibility of further help available to the client (my therapy demonstrations discussed in Chapter 7 being one such example) – but in the main SST is best offered when integrated with other modes of therapy delivery so that people who require more than one session can be quickly seen.

Sometimes it is clear that the person does not need more than a single therapy session and sometimes it is clear that they do need more help. When both the therapist and client are unsure about this point, the therapist might usefully encourage the client to reflect on what they have learned from the session, digest the learning, take action and let time pass before deciding whether or not to seek further help.

It is important to recognise at the outset that single-session therapy is neither a therapeutic technique nor a therapeutic approach. Rather, SST is best seen as a mindset and a mode of therapy delivery, as I will discuss later in this chapter

It is based on the idea that a brief encounter between people can be therapeutic for one of them and on the idea that the length of therapy is expandable. As Moshe Talmon (1993: 135) stated: 'Therapy takes exactly the length of time allocated for it. When the therapist and client expect change to happen now, it often does.'

The foundations of single-session therapy

Young (2018) argued that there are three foundations of single-session therapy:

- In public and charitable therapy agencies worldwide, the modal[1] number of therapy sessions that people have is '1', followed by '2', followed by '3', etc. (e.g. Brown & Jones, 2005).
- Between 70% and 80% of clients who have one session are satisfied with that session given their current circumstances (Campbell, 2012; Talmon, 1990).
- Therapists are poor at predicting who will attend for only one session and who will attend for more, a proposition that has significant clinical and organisational ramifications.

These foundations show that clients often, but not always, are looking to be helped briefly, frequently in one session, and that, contrary to the views of clinicians, satisfaction levels in SST are high, so, since therapists cannot predict the attendance patterns of clients, why not offer everyone a single session and see what happens? It is important to remember that SST does not mean that further help is not available.

Help provided at the point of need

The current efforts of mental health professionals, aided by members of the Royal Family and sporting and entertainment celebrities, to destigmatise mental health issues are to be applauded. 'Seek help for these issues' is a natural follow-on message, and yet when people do come forward for help, they often have to wait for it, sometimes for what seems like an inordinate amount of time. This is known as 'help provided at the point of availability'. An agency provides help when it is able to do so. This is usually because such agencies offer people who manage to see a counsellor as much help as they need or blocks of counselling sessions, the most common number in these blocks being '6'.[2]

An alternative to 'help provided at the point of availability' is 'help provided at the point of need'. Such help can be provided by walk-in or by appointment.

SST by walk-in

It is important to distinguish between a 'walk-in' service and a 'drop-in' service. A walk-in service offers a person therapy from moment one and is staffed by professionals trained in SST. A 'drop-in' service, on the other hand, tends to offer a person a chat, support and signposting information and is staffed by those without professional training in SST. A walk-in service 'enables clients to meet with a mental health professional at their moment of choosing. There is no red tape, no triage, no intake process, no wait list, and no wait. There is no formal assessment, no formal diagnostic process, just one hour of therapy focused on clients' stated wants...Also, with walk-in therapy there are no missed appointments or cancellations, thereby increasing efficiency.' (Slive, McElheran & Lawson, 2008 :6).

SST by appointment

In addition to SST by walk-in, SST can also be delivered by appointment. For a client to experience the potency of SST, it is important for the person to be seen as soon as possible after making an appointment. Even then, it is important for the person to make good use of the time between making an appointment for SST and having the session by preparing for the session.

Ideas underpinning help provided at the point of need

Help provided at the point of need is based on the following ideas:

- It is better to respond to client need by providing some help straightaway rather than by waiting to provide them with the best possible help. However, the client can choose to wait for this latter help if they know how long the wait will be.
- Providing immediate help is more important than carrying out a full assessment or a case formulation.
- Therapy can be initiated in the absence of a case history.
- People have the resources to make use of help provided at the point of need.
- Sooner is better.
- The best way to see if a client will respond well to therapy is by offering them therapy and seeing how they respond.
- Therapy can be initiated and risk managed if this becomes an issue.
- Appropriate therapy length is best determined by the client.
- When a person does not return for another session, this may well indicate that the person is satisfied with what they achieved, although it may be the case that they were dissatisfied with the help provided.

The goals of single-session therapy

What can be realistically achieved from a single session of therapy? My view is SST can help a client in a number of ways. It can help the client to:

- Get 'unstuck' when they are stuck with a particular issue or problem. This often happens when the person has been applying a strategy which only serves to maintain the problem. Encouraging the client to find a different strategy often helps them to get unstuck.

- Take a few steps forward which may help them to travel the rest of the journey without professional assistance. People often need a helping hand to move forward, particularly if they are encouraged to use their strengths in the process.
- Address a specific concern. Here, the single-session therapist will help the person to focus on the concern, explore potential solutions and select the one that seems the best available that the person can implement in their life. Then the person can be helped to practise the solution in the session and to develop an action plan to aid implementation.
- Explore an issue in order to get greater clarity. While SST often involves focused interventions, sometimes when a client wants to get greater clarity on an issue, SST can help them to achieve this by adopting an exploratory and clarifying role.

Who is suitable for SST?

One of the most frequently asked questions about SST concerns client suitability. This may, at first sight, be a perfectly sensible question. Indeed, it is one that I grappled with myself when I first became interested in SST and formulated my own approach which I called Single-Session Integrated Cognitive-Behaviour Therapy (Dryden, 2017).

Developing lists of inclusion and exclusion criteria

What I did was to develop a long list of indications and contraindications for SSI-CBT and then I had a light-bulb moment. I realised that what I was doing was developing a single-session assessment protocol to determine who could and could not benefit from single-session therapy. I also realised that what I was doing was against the spirit of single-session therapy, where the emphasis is on offering therapy at first contact rather than assessment at first contact. So, while the suitability question seems a useful question to ask, it isn't.

Walk-in

As noted above, the idea behind walk-in therapy services is that a person is able to 'walk in' to a therapy centre and receive one session of therapy with minimum bureaucracy and minimum wait. In effect, the person themself is judging that they are suitable for receiving help for their pressing concern and the therapist also proceeds on this assumption. In effect, people go to a walk-in service for a variety of reasons. They may do so even if their problems are serious, chronic and complex. However, because the focus of a single session is on their most pressing concern, they can and do derive benefit from SST.

So, as noted above, the best answer to the question concerning whether a person will benefit from a single session of therapy is for them to have a session of therapy and discover the answer to the question from their actual experience, not from a predetermined set of inclusion and exclusion criteria.

If, as a result of what transpires in the walk-in session, it turns out that the person requires a different form of help or more sessions, this is discussed with the person who is free to determine how to proceed. While a person may walk back in for another walk-in session and is free to do so, most people do not do this.

Client choice, refer to other services if necessary

Single-session therapy is best located alongside other modes of therapy delivery within an agency. When this happens, the agency usually lists the services that they offer on their website. Thus, another way of determining whether or not a person is suitable for SST is to permit a person to make the decision that SST best suits their needs and let them have the single session. If they benefit from the session, all well and good; if they do not, then they can be referred to one of the other services that the agency offers or to a different agency.

The 'embedded' approach

Perhaps the best answer to the suitability question can be found in the work of the Bouverie Centre, a family therapy institute in Victoria, Australia. As described by Young (2018), everybody who seeks help from the Bouverie Centre is offered a single session of therapy, the objective of which is to see if the clients and therapists can work together to solve the problem in that session. If not, further help is available in the form of another single session, more ongoing sessions or a specialised service. The Bouverie Centre knows from the statistics they have collated over the years that, for about half of the clients who receive a single session, that session is sufficient for their need at that time. The other clients receive other services offered by the Centre.

All this is done without any pre-therapy assessment. If such assessment were to be done, it would significantly increase the waiting time between the clients applying for and receiving help. In this way, the suitability issue is dealt with by effectively not being dealt with.

The single-session therapy mindset and implications for good practice

As I made clear earlier in this chapter, single-session therapy is neither a technique nor an approach to therapy in the way that cognitive-behaviour therapy or narrative therapy is. It is both a mode of therapy delivery and a mindset with pantheoretical implications for good practice. In this section, I will discuss the latter.

Utilise 'now'

Single-session therapy is predicated on the idea that all we have is 'now' and therefore it is important for the therapist to ask themself what they want to do with the client given this fact. Do they want to assess the person's suitability for a range of possible services? Do they want to undertake a full assessment of the client and their problems? Do they want to carry out a case formulation? Do they want to gather a case history? Or do they want to offer the client a therapy session from moment one? The single-session practitioner's decided answer is the latter. They argue that since we do not know for certain if a client is going to return, why not proceed on the basis that this may be the only opportunity to help the client and, as such, beginning therapy is the best way of doing this.

Create a realistic expectation for SST

As discussed in the section on the goals of SST, this mode of therapy delivery can help the client take away something meaningful from the session that they can implement in their life in the area of the client's most pressing concern. If they can also be shown how to generalise this learning to other areas of their life, then so much the better, but the therapist needs to focus on what can be realistically achieved from the session and guard against being too ambitious in aiming to help the client take away *too* much from the session.

On the other hand, therapists who think that nothing much can be achieved from a single session will help the client achieve just that – nothing much. If some clients aren't suitable for SST, the same is true for some therapists. Thus, creating realistic expectations for SST lies in the fertile ground between 'nothing much can be achieved' and 'wanting the client to take away too much from the session to apply across the board'.

Client-centred

Therapists are generally trained not only to consider what the client brings but also to identify what might underlie what the client brings. When I was trained as a counsellor in the mid-1970s, much was made of the distinction between the client's presenting problem and their real problem. The language used made it quite clear what therapists thought of the status of the presenting problem. The mindset of the single-session therapist is quite different on this point. It is to take seriously what the client identifies as their most pressing concern and to focus their joint attention on this issue with the intention of finding a solution to it. This shows the client-centred nature of single-session thinking and practice.

Engage the client quickly through the work

Perhaps one of the most frequently expressed reservations about SST by therapists concerns the therapeutic relationship. Their argument is that as the therapeutic relationship takes time to develop, it is not possible for the therapist to form a relationship with the client in SST to enable them to help the client in such a short period of time. However, this is not borne out by research. For example, Simon, Imel, Ludman and Steinfeld's (2012) found that clients benefiting from SST reported a strong working alliance with their therapists, while clients not benefiting from SST reported a weak alliance with their therapists. Such research shows that it is entirely possible to form a good working relationship with clients quickly. What are the ingredients of such a relationship?

In my view, the single-session therapist develops a good working relationship with the client by a) showing them that they are keen to help them as quickly as possible; b) communicating that they understand them from their frame of reference; c) demonstrating that they take their nominated most pressing concern seriously; and d) helping them to set a goal for the session which they work with them to achieve.

The concept of working at relational depth with clients is popular at the moment with counsellors and psychotherapists (Mearns & Cooper, 2018). SST therapists would question the clinical wisdom of working at relational depth with *some* clients. However, they argue that for *other* clients working at relational promptness[3] is equally important.

Ask the client how they best want to be helped

While focusing on a pressing issue and looking for a solution to this issue is perhaps the most common feature of SST, it is not the only feature of this work. Sometimes a client may wish to explore an issue or seek to understand it with greater clarity, and it is thus important for the therapist to be flexible about which helping stance to adopt with a client. The client may provide information about what type of help they are looking for in response to a question about what led them to seek a single session or in response to a question about what they want to achieve by the end of the session. However, perhaps the best questions on this point are as follows:

- How can I best help you today?
- What approach can I take with you today that you would find most helpful?

If the client is unsure about how to respond, then the therapist might give them a number of alternatives and stress that these are all equally acceptable:

- Some clients find it most useful when I help them to focus on their most pressing concern and we work together to find a solution to the problem.
- Some clients prefer to use the session to explore an issue without needing to find a solution and I help them to do this.

- Some clients are seeking clarity or understanding on an issue and I work to help them to achieve this.
- Some clients are looking for help to make a decision and I will help them to do this.
- Some clients just want an opportunity to talk and for me to listen to them and I am happy to do this.

Develop and work towards an end-of-session goal

In therapy that extends over time, if a therapist adopts a goal-taking perspective[4] at the outset, they will ask a question such as: 'What would you like to achieve at the end of therapy?' This reflects the therapist's 'ongoing therapy' mindset. In SST, where the focus is on helping the client in one session while recognising that more help may be available, the emphasis is very different and the therapist will ask a question such as: 'What would you like to achieve by the end of the session?' This reflects the therapist's 'single-session therapy' mindset.

Agree a focus for the session

Whether a client wants help in finding a solution to a problem, in exploring an issue, in gaining greater understanding of an issue or in making a decision (amongst other things), it is important that the therapist helps the client to agree a focus for the session. The exception to this is where the person wants to talk in an uninterrupted way and wants the therapist to listen to them. In such a case, the therapist will show listening attention while the client talks about whatever they wish to talk about.

Keep on track

Once a focus has been agreed, it is the therapist's task to help the client to keep on track, checking from time to time whether they are discussing what the person most wants to talk about.

To help the client to keep to their agreed focus, it is important for the therapist to interrupt the client but to do so with tact. In my experience, therapists find doing this difficult either because they have been trained not to interfere with the client's process or because they think that it is rude to interrupt a client. The first point reflects a therapist's 'ongoing therapy' mindset, which may be suited to ongoing therapy but is not generally helpful in SST, where a different mindset is called for which stresses the importance of creating and keeping to an agreed focus. The second point confuses action with style. In my view, the action of interrupting a client is not inherently rude. Thus, my way of doing this is to say to a client at the outset, 'During the session, I may need to interrupt you to help us keep on track. Do I have your permission to do this?' I aver that this is not rude, particularly if the client agrees to me doing this, which they invariably do. So, the act of interrupting a client is in itself not rude, but *how* a therapist does this may be rude.

Use good pacing

A single session of therapy usually lasts the same length of time as any other session of psychotherapy.[5] Some therapists are time-aware in a constructive manner, take the time frame in their stride and carry out the session in a focused, well-paced manner. Other therapists are time-anxious and conduct the session in a rushed and what seems like a frenetic manner. It is not surprising that the former group is often more effective than the latter.

The former group can be identified by two markers. First, they think that a therapy session is sufficiently long to do good work. Second, they strive to do as much as they can in the session, hoping that the client will take away something meaningful from the session, without demanding that this happens.

The latter group can also be identified by the presence of two markers. First, they think that a therapy session is an insufficient amount of time to get the job done without rushing. Second, they demand that they have to help the client take away something meaningful from the session. Helping this group of therapists to see that they have longer than they think they have in SST and to be flexible in their attitude towards what clients take away from the session will usually result in these therapists using better pacing in their single sessions.

Be clear

Therapist clarity is a crucial feature of effective SST in my view and should permeate the session. Thus, the therapist should be clear about the following:

- the purpose of the session as they see it
- what they can do as a therapist and what they can't do
- what further help is available to the client, if any, and how this help can be accessed
- the reason why they may need to interrupt the client (see above)
- the rationale behind any major interventions
- any concepts that they need to explain to the client (e.g. acceptance, mindfulness).

If the therapist is unsure that they are being clear, then it is useful for them to ask the client if the client would put their understanding of what the therapist said into their own words.

Make an emotional impact, if possible

For the client to get the most out of a single session they need to be both emotionally engaged and cognitively engaged in the session. I refer to this as 'head and heart working together'. Thus, the therapist needs to look for and use opportunities to make an emotional impact on the client so that the latter can process what they discuss in the session in a way that facilitates change. If the client's emotions are not engaged in what they are discussing, then the therapeutic pair will have a nice theoretical discussion which will not lead to any therapeutic change. On the other hand, if the client is flooded with emotion to the extent that they can't think, then this will not lead to change either.

Identify and utilise client strengths and values

In one hour of therapy, it is not likely that the therapist will be able to teach the client skills that are not already in their repertoire. So the therapist will need to help the client to use what they do have in their repertoire. This involves the therapist helping the client to identify those strengths that they have which they can use to address their problem or issue. Examples of such strengths include perseverance, resilience, intelligence and empathy. It also involves the therapist helping the client to identify and let themself be guided by their values. Examples of such values include open-mindedness, honesty, loyalty and dependability.

You might be thinking what is the difference between strengths and values. For me, values give direction to a person's goals, while the person draws on their strengths to help them to achieve these goals (see Figure 8.1). As such, both a client's strengths and their values are useful resources in SST.

Figure 8.1   Strengths, values and goals

Encourage the client to use external resources

In addition to drawing on the client's internal resources (strengths and values) in SST, the therapist also encourages the client to identify and use their external resources to help them with their nominated problem/issue. A good example of such an external resource is people on the client's 'team' who may help them or support them as they work towards dealing with their nominated issue. Here, different people may offer different types of help, as is the case with those involved with a professional tennis player (e.g. 'Team Murray'). Other examples of external resources include organisations that offer help, phone 'apps' that may assist the client in some way and, of course, a variety of search engines on the internet.

Identify and utilise the client's previous attempts to deal with the problem

If the client has come to SST hoping to deal with a specific concern, it is likely that they have tried to deal with it or sought help from friends and relatives before seeking professional help. The single-session therapist seeks to discover what the person has done to help themself with their problem and the outcome of such endeavours, encouraging the person to capitalise on what they have found helpful in the past and to cast aside what was unhelpful.

Negotiate a solution

Particularly if the person is seeking help with a problem, the main task of the SST practitioner is to help them to find a 'solution' to this problem. In SST, I conceptualise a solution as that which effectively addresses the client's problem so that they can work towards achieving their problem-related goal.

There are two types of SST practitioners: 'problem/solution-focused' and 'solution-focused'. The former type will tend to help the client identify their most pressing problem and what they consider to be a goal with respect to this problem. They will help the client to identify a solution which effectively addresses the problem

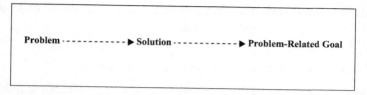

Figure 8.2   The relation between problem, solution and problem-related goal in problem/solution-focused SST

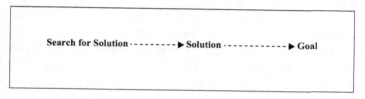

Figure 8.3   The relation between solution and goal in solution-focused SST

and helps them to achieve their goal (see Figure 8.2). In this approach to SST, while the therapist will help the client to identify a goal with respect to their nominated problem, they will also help them, as previously noted, to identify an end-of-session goal. When done well, the end-of-session goal is, in effect, the same as the solution. Here the client knows that they still have to implement the solution in their everyday life and is prepared to develop an action plan to do so with the help of the therapist (see below).

The latter type will help the client focus on a solution that will help the person do the same, but without the problem focus. For the latter therapists, the work will be different, as shown in Figure 8.3.

This section's heading uses the term 'negotiate' a solution. The task of client and therapist here is to consider possible solutions to the client's problem and for the client to select the one that is most likely to solve it and that they are most likely to implement. Both should share any reservations they have about any of the proposed solutions and work them through until they agree which solution the client is going to take forward.

Encourage the client to rehearse the solution

Once the client has chosen a solution, then the therapist should encourage them to rehearse it in the session to determine whether or not the solution resonates with them and to identify any problems that they may have implementing it in their life. In the same way as a person will want to test drive a car before committing to buying it, a client should test drive or rehearse a solution before committing to using it. After rehearsing a solution, the client will decide either to take it forward, perhaps after tweaking it, or not to use it. In the latter case, the therapist and client will select a different solution on the basis of the reasons why the client rejected the first.

Methods that a therapist might suggest that a client use while rehearsing a solution include imagery, role-play and chair-work.

Help the client to develop an action plan

In the section on 'negotiate a solution', I made reference to an 'action plan'. This involves the therapist helping the client to determine where they are going to implement the situation, when they are going to implement it and what resources they will need to implement it. In addition, it is useful if the therapist can help the client to identify any obstacles to implementing the solution and work with the client to prevent the obstacles from occurring or to deal with them effectively if they do occur.

Encourage the client to summarise

As the end of the session approaches, it is a good idea for the therapist to encourage the client to summarise the session from their perspective. While therapists are accustomed to using summarising at various junctures in ongoing therapy, asking the client to summarise the session ensures that the client remains active in the session even at its end, and more importantly ensures that the client will take away the points outlined in their summary rather than those that might feature in the therapist's summary. Having said that, the therapist should feel free to add to the client's summary if they feel that the client has omitted an important point.

Encourage the client to take away 'one thing'

It is important that the therapist does not overload the client during the session; if they do, it is likely that the client will not take anything away from it. In a business context, Keller and Papasan (2012) argue that by focusing on one task a person will achieve more than if they focus on two or more tasks. As the saying goes, 'if you chase two rabbits, you will catch neither'. If the client mentions more than one key point that they will take away from the session, it is useful if the client links these points together so that the 'one thing' principle is preserved.

Encourage the use of the reflect–digest–act–wait–decide process

As mentioned earlier, in SST the therapist and the client work together with the intention of helping the client in that session on the understanding that more sessions are available if needed. If the client is unsure if they require any more help at the end of the session, then the therapist can encourage them to engage in a five-step process whereby after the session the client reflects on what they have learned from the session, digests this learning, acts on it and lets time pass before deciding whether or not they require more help.

Tie up loose ends and clarify next steps

Frank (1961) argued that people often seek help because they are in a state of demoralisation. It follows, therefore, that a major goal of psychotherapy is to restore their morale. While doing this in SST is a challenge for the therapist, it is one that the single-session practitioner is prepared to take on. While the bulk of the session is devoted to achieving this, it is also important that at the very end of the session the therapist ties up any loose ends with the client. This involves the client being encouraged to say anything at the end of the session that they may later regret not saying and to ask any questions that they may later regret not asking. The goal here is for the client to leave the session with a sense of closure and completion and with their morale sufficiently restored so that they look towards the future with increased hope.

As part of this process, it is important that the client is clear about how they can access more help should they need to in the future.

Arrange follow-up, if possible

SST purists argue that this mode of therapy delivery involves one session and no other contact – no pre-session contact to help the client to prepare for the session and no follow-up session. However, in this day and age when therapists need to show the effectiveness of their interventions, it is unrealistic for a follow-up session not to be held, assuming that it is practicable for this to be arranged. For how else are therapists to know whether SST is effective and what clients think of the service that they have received so that they can improve what they offer to clients?

Afterword

While SST has reinvigorated my therapeutic career, it has also helped me be more efficient and effective in my non-SST practice. Thus, I am more attuned to helping clients achieve what they want to achieve from each session than I used to be, and I am more efficient than hitherto in my use of session time. I also encourage my clients to prepare for each session, to focus on a main 'takeaway' from each session and to reflect, digest, take action and then wait to decide if they want to make another appointment to see me. I have learned all this from the SST literature. Of course, some clients need the security of having regular sessions, but even with these clients I stress the importance of session preparation and reflection.

On this note, we have reached the end of the book. In it I have outlined those ideas that have most influenced me in what has been a long and varied career in the field of counselling and psycho-therapy – 45 years to date. However, my career is not at an end quite yet and who knows which ideas may influence me going forward? Finally, I welcome feedback on this book at windy@windydryden.com

Notes

1 The mode is the most frequently occurring number in a series.
2 I have yet to be given an evidence-based answer for why there should be six sessions in a block rather than five or seven sessions, for example.
3 By 'relational promptness' I mean the therapist developing an effective working alliance with a client quickly in the first and perhaps only session that the two people will have together.
4 Some therapists do not think it is helpful to ask a client about their therapeutic goals, and some will wait to do so until they understand the client and their problems better.
5 There are exceptions. Some family therapists devote more time to a session in SST than they do to a session in ongoing therapy. In a single-session, exposure-based approach to the treatment of simple phobias, the session can last up to three hours (Zlomke & Davis, 2008).

Appendix

An example of Dr Albert Ellis using the 'Money Model' to explain the REBT model of psychological disturbance

Ellis: Imagine that you prefer to have a minimum of $11 in your pocket at all times, but it's not necessary that you have this amount. If you discover you only have $10, how will you feel?

Client: Frustrated.

Ellis: Right. Or you'd feel concerned or sad, but you wouldn't kill yourself. Right?

Client: Right.

Ellis: OK. Now this time imagine that you absolutely <u>have to</u> have a minimum $11 in your pocket at all times. You <u>must</u> have it, it is a <u>necessity</u>. You <u>must</u>, you <u>must</u>, you <u>must</u> have a minimum of $11, and again you look and you find you only have $10. How will you feel?

Client: Very anxious.

Ellis: Right, or depressed. Now remember it's the same $10, but a different belief. OK, now this time you still have the same belief. You <u>have to</u> have a minimum of $11 at all times, you <u>must</u>. It's absolutely <u>essential</u>. But this time you look in your pocket and find that you've got $15. How will you feel?

Client: Relieved, content.

Ellis: Right. But with that same belief, you <u>have to</u> have a minimum of $11 at all times – something will occur to you to scare you shitless. What do you think that would be?

Client: What if I lose $5?

Ellis: Right. What if I lose $5, what if I spend $5, what if I get robbed? That's right. Now the moral of this model – which applies to just about all humans, rich or poor, black or white, male or female, young or old, in the past or in the future, assuming humans are still human – is that people <u>make them-selves</u> miserable if they don't get what they think they <u>must</u> get, but they are also panicked when they do get what they think they <u>must</u> get – because of the must. For even if they have what they think they must have, they could always lose it.

Client: So, I have no chance to be happy when I don't have what I think I <u>must</u> have – and little chance of remaining unanxious when I do have it?

Ellis: Right! Your <u>mus</u>turbation will get you nowhere – except depressed or panicked!

Source: Reproduced from Ellis and Dryden (1997: 40–41) in slightly modified form with permission from Springer Publishing Co, New York.

References

Baldwin, S.A., & Imel, Z.E. (2013). Therapist effects: Findings and methods. In M.J. Lambert, *Bergin and Garfield's handbook of psychotherapy and behavior change, 6th edition*. New York: Wiley.

Barker, C., Pistrang, N., Shapiro, D.A., & Shaw, I. (1990). Coping and help-seeking in the UK adult population. *British Journal of Clinical Psychology, 29*, 271–285.

Beck, A.T. (1976). *Cognitive therapy and the emotional disorders*. New York: International Universities Press.

Beck, A.T., Rush, A.J., Shaw, B.F., & Emery, G. (1979). *Cognitive therapy of depression*. New York: Guilford.

Berne, E. (1957). Ego states in psychotherapy. *American Journal of Psychotherapy, 11*, 293–309.

Beutler, L.E., Malik, M., Alimohammed, S., Harwood, T.M., Talebi, H., Noble, S., & Wong, E. (2004). Therapist variables. In M.J. Lambert, *Bergin and Garfield's handbook of psychotherapy and behavior change, 5th edition* (pp. 227–306). New York: Wiley.

Bond, F.W., & Dryden, W. (1996). Modifying irrational control and certainty beliefs: Clinical recommendations based upon research. In W. Dryden (Ed.), *Research in counselling and psychotherapy: Practical applications* (pp. 162–183). London: Sage.

Bordin, E.S. (1979). The generalizability of the psychoanalytic concept of the working alliance. *Psychotherapy, 16*, 252–260.

Bordin, E.S. (1983). A working alliance based model of supervision. *Counseling Psychologist, 11*, 35–42.

Brattland, H., Koksvik, J.M., Burkeland, O., Klöckner, C.A., Lara-Cabrera, M.L., Miller, S.D., Wampold, B., Ryum, T., & Iversen, V.C. (2019). Does the working alliance mediate the effect of routine outcome monitoring (ROM) and alliance feedback on psychotherapy outcomes? A secondary analysis from a randomized clinical trial. *Journal of Counseling Psychology, 66*, 234–246.

Brown, G.S., & Jones, E.R. (2005). Implementation of a feedback system in a managed care environment: What are patients teaching us? *Journal of Clinical Psychology, 61*, 187–198.

Burns, D.D. (1980). *Feeling good: The new mood therapy.* New York: Morrow.

Campbell, A. (2012). Single-session approaches to therapy: Time to review. *Australian and New Zealand Journal of Family Therapy, 33*(1), 15–26.

Colman, A. (2015). *Oxford dictionary of psychology, 4th edition.* Oxford: Oxford University Press.

Constantino, M.J., Ladany, N., & Borkovec, T.D. (2010). Edward S. Bordin: Innovative thinker, influential investigator, and inspiring teacher. In L.G. Castonguay, J.C. Muran, L. Angus, J.A. Hayes, N. Ladany & T. Anderson (Eds.), *Bringing psychotherapy research to life: Understanding change through the work of leading clinical researchers* (pp. 21–57). Washington, DC: American Psychological Association.

Cooper, M., & Dryden, W. (Eds.). (2016). *The handbook of pluralistic counselling and psychotherapy.* London: Sage.

Cooper, M., & McLeod, J. (2011). *Pluralistic counselling and psychotherapy.* London: Sage.

Dorn, F.J. (Ed.). (1984). *The social influence process in counseling and psychotherapy.* Springfield, IL: Charles C. Thomas.

Dryden, W. (1982). The therapeutic alliance: Conceptual issues and some research findings. *Midland Journal of Psychotherapy, 1* (June), 14–19.

Dryden, W. (1986). Some aspects of the therapeutic alliance in rational-emotive therapy. *British Journal of Cognitive Psychotherapy, 4*(2), 78–82.

Dryden, W. (1987). Compromises in rational-emotive therapy. In W. Dryden, *Current issues in rational-emotive therapy* (pp. 72–87). London: Croom Helm.

Dryden, W. (1989). The therapeutic alliance as an integrating framework. In W. Dryden (Ed.), *Key issues for counselling in action* (pp. 1–15). London: Sage Publications.

Dryden, W. (1996). *Rational emotive behaviour therapy: Learning from demonstration sessions.* London: Whurr Publishers.

Dryden, W. (2001). My idiosyncratic practice of REBT. *Romanian Journal of Cognitive and Behavioral Psychotherapies, 1*(1), 17–30.

Dryden, W. (Ed.). (2002a). *Idiosyncratic rational emotive behaviour therapy.* Ross-on-Wye: PCCS Books.

Dryden, W. (2002b). The Florence Nightingale Hospital CBT group therapy programme. In W. Dryden & M. Neenan (Eds.), *Rational emotive behaviour group therapy* (pp. 106–123). London: Whurr.

Dryden, W. (2006). *Counselling in a nutshell.* London: Sage.

Dryden, W. (2009). *How to think and intervene like an REBT therapist.* Hove, East Sussex: Routledge.

Dryden, W. (2010a). Elegance in REBT: Reflections on the Ellis and Dryden sessions with Jane. *Journal of Rational-Emotive and Cognitive-Behavior Therapy, 28*(3), 157–163.

Dryden, W. (2010b). Two REBT therapists and one client: Windy Dryden transcript. *Journal of Rational-Emotive and Cognitive-Behavior Therapy, 28*(3), 130–140.

Dryden, W. (2011). *Counselling in a nutshell, 2nd edition.* London: Sage.

Dryden, W. (2012). *Dealing with emotional problems using rational-emotive cognitive behaviour therapy: A practitioner's guide.* Hove, East Sussex: Routledge.

Dryden, W. (2013). *The ABCs of REBT: Perspectives on conceptualization.* New York: Springer.

Dryden, W. (2014). Rational emotive behaviour therapy. In W. Dryden & A. Reeves (Eds.), *The handbook of individual therapy, 6th edition* (pp. 271–299). London: Sage.

Dryden, W. (2016). *Attitudes in rational emotive behaviour therapy: Components, characteristics and adversity-related consequences.* London: Rationality Publications.

Dryden, W. (2017). *Single-session integrated CBT (SSI-CBT): Distinctive features.* Abingdon, Oxon: Routledge.

Dryden, W., & Ellis, A. (2003). *Albert Ellis live!* London: Sage.

Dryden, W., DiGiuseppe, R., & Neenan, M. (2010). *A primer on rational emotive behavior therapy, 3rd edition.* Champaign, IL: Research Press.

Dryden, W., Ferguson, J., & Clark, A. (1989). Beliefs and inferences: A test of a rational-emotive hypothesis, 1: Performing in an academic seminar. *Journal of Rational-Emotive and Cognitive Behavior Therapy, 7,* 119–129.

Dryden, W., Ferguson, J., & Hylton, B. (1989). Beliefs and inferences: A test of a rational-emotive hypothesis, 3: On expectations about enjoying a party. *British Journal of Guidance & Counselling, 17,* 68–75.

Dryden, W., Ferguson, J., & McTeague, S. (1989). Beliefs and inferences: A test of a rational-emotive hypothesis, 2: On the prospect of seeing a spider. *Psychological Reports, 64,* 115–123.

Eagly, A.H., & Chaiken, S. (1993). *The psychology of attitudes.* Fort Worth, TX: Harcourt Brace Jovanovich College Publishers.

Ellis, A. (1958). Rational psychotherapy. *Journal of General Psychology, 59,* 35–49.

Ellis, A. (1959). Requisite conditions for basic personality change. *Journal of Consulting Psychology, 23,* 538–540.

Ellis, A. (1971). *Growth through reason: Verbatim cases in rational-emotive therapy.* Palo Alto, CA: Science & Behavior.

Ellis, A. (1972). Helping people get better rather than merely feel better. *Rational Living, 7*(2), 2–9.

Ellis, A. (1976). The biological basis of human irrationality. *Journal of Individual Psychology, 32,* 145–168.

Ellis, A. (1983). *The case against religiosity.* New York: Institute for Rational-Emotive Therapy.

Ellis, A., & Dryden, W. (1987). *The practice of rational-emotive therapy.* New York: Springer.

Ellis, A., & Dryden, W. (1997). *The practice of rational emotive behavior therapy, 2nd edition.* New York: Springer.

Ellis, A., & Joffe, D. (2002). A study of volunteer clients who experienced live sessions of rational emotive behavior therapy in front of a public audience. *Journal of Rational-Emotive & Cognitive-Behavior Therapy, 20,* 151–158.

Ellis, A., & Joffe Ellis, D. (2011). *Rational emotive behavior therapy.* Washington, DC: American Psychological Association.

Frank, J.D. (1961). *Persuasion and healing: A comprehensive study of psychotherapy.* Baltimore, MD: Johns Hopkins Press.

Frankl, V. (1984). *Man's search for meaning.* New York: Washington Square Press.

Freud, S. (1961). *The ego and the id.* New York: W.W. Norton & Co.

Frijda, N.H. (1993). The place of appraisal in emotion. *Cognition and Emotion, 7,* 357–388.

Frijda, N.H. (1995). Passions: Emotions and socially consequential behavior. In R.D. Kavanaugh, B. Zimmerberg & S. Fein (Eds.), *Emotion: Interdisciplinary perspectives* (pp. 1–28). Mahwah, NJ: Erlbaum.

Gabbard, G. (2001). Psychotherapy in Hollywood cinema. *Australasian Psychiatry, 9,* 365–369.

Hauck, P.A. (1980). *Brief counseling with RET.* Philadelphia, PA: Westminster Press.

Hobson, R.F. (1985). *Forms of feeling: The heart of psychotherapy.* London: Tavistock Publications.

Hogg, M., & Vaughan, G. (2005). *Social psychology, 4th edition.* London: Prentice-Hall.

Hoyt, M.F., Bobele, M., Slive, A., Young, J., & Talmon, M. (2018). Introduction: One-at-a-time/single-session walk-in therapy. In M.F. Hoyt, M. Bobele, A. Slive, J. Young & M. Talmon (Eds.), *Single-session therapy by walk-in or appointment: Administrative, clinical, and supervisory aspects of one-at-a time services* (pp. 3–24). New York: Routledge.

Hoyt, M.F., & Talmon, M.F. (2014). What the literature says: An annotated bibliography. In M.F. Hoyt & M. Talmon (Eds.), *Capturing the moment: Single session therapy and walk-in services* (pp. 487–516). Bethel, CT: Crown House Publishing.

Keller, G., & Papasan, J. (2012). *The one thing: The surprisingly simple truth behind extraordinary results.* Austin, TX: Bard Press.

Keys, S. (Ed.). (2003). *Idiosyncratic practice of person-centred therapy: From the personal to the universal.* Ross-on-Wye: PCCS Books.

Law, D., & Jacob. J. (2015). *Goals and goal based outcomes (GBOs): Some useful information, 3rd edition.* London: CAMHS Press.

Lazarus, A. (1989). *The practice of multimodal therapy.* Baltimore, MD: Johns Hopkins University Press.

Lazarus, A. (1993). Tailoring the therapeutic relationship, or being an authentic chameleon. *Psychotherapy: Theory, Research, Practice, Training, 30*(3), 404–407.

Mahrer, A. (Ed.). (1967). *The goals of psychotherapy.* Englewood Cliffs, NJ: Prentice-Hall.

Maluccio, A.N. (1979). *Learning from clients: Interpersonal helping as viewed by clients and social workers.* New York: Free Press.

Mearns, D., & Cooper, M. (2018). *Working at relational depth in counselling and psychotherapy, 2nd edition.* London: Sage.

Nolen-Hoeksema, S., Wisco, B.E., & Lyubomirsky, S. (2008). Rethinking rumination. *Perspectives on Psychological Science, 3*, 400–424.

Orsillo, S.M., & Roemer, L. (Eds.). (2005). *Acceptance and mindfulness-based approaches to anxiety: Conceptualization and treatment.* New York: Springer.

Pistrang, N., & Barker, C. (1992). Clients' beliefs about psychological problems. *Counselling Psychology Quarterly, 5*, 325–336.

Rescher, N. (1993). *Pluralism: Against the demand for consensus.* Oxford: Oxford University Press.

Rogers, C.R. (1942). *Counseling and psychotherapy: Newer concepts in practice.* Boston, MA: Houghton Mifflin.

Rogers, C.R. (1957). The necessary and sufficient conditions of therapeutic personality change. *Journal of Consulting Psychology, 21,* 95–103.

Safran, J.D., & Muran, J.C. (2000). Resolving therapeutic alliance ruptures: Diversity and integration. *Journal of Clinical Psychology/In Session, 56,* 233–243.

Simon, G.E., Imel, Z.E., Ludman, E.J., & Steinfeld, B.J. (2012). Is dropout after a first psychotherapy visit always a bad outcome? *Psychiatric Services, 63*(7), 705–707.

Slive, A., McElheran, N., & Lawson, A. (2008). How brief does it get? Walk-in single session therapy. *Journal of Systemic Therapies, 27,* 5–22.

Sterba, R. (1934). The fate of the ego in analytic therapy. *International Journal of Psychoanalysis, 15,* 117–126.

Talmon, M. (1990). *Single session therapy: Maximising the effect of the first (and often only) therapeutic encounter.* San Francisco, CA: Jossey-Bass.

Talmon, M. (1993). *Single session solutions: A guide to practical, effective and affordable therapy.* New York: Addison-Wesley.

Wegner, D.M. (1989). *White bears and other unwanted thoughts: Suppression, obsession, and the psychology of mental control.* New York: Guilford.

Wegner, D.M., & Schneider, D.J. (2003). The white bear story. *Psychological Inquiry, 14,* 326–329.

Young, J. (2018). SST: The misunderstood gift that keeps on giving. In M.F. Hoyt, M. Bobele, A. Slive, J. Young, & M. Talmon (Eds.), *Single-session therapy by walk-in or appointment: Administrative, clinical, and supervisory aspects of one-at-a time services* (pp. 40–58). New York: Routledge.

Zlomke, K., & Davis, T.E. (2008). One-session treatment of specific phobias: A detailed description and review of treatment efficacy. *Behavior Therapy, 39,* 207–223.

Index

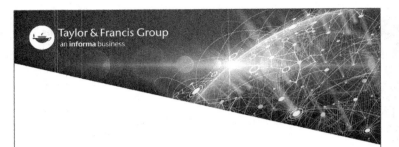

Printed in the United States
by Baker & Taylor Publisher Services